Hippocrene U.S.A. Guide to

BLACK NEW YORK

1082047 28

D1520066

About the Authors

Jim Haskins is professor of English at the University of Florida in Gainesville. He is the author of over 80 books about black culture in America including the *Psychology of Black Language* and *The Cotton Club*. He lives in Florida and New York City.

Joann Biondi is a freelance writer and author of five travel books. Her articles have appeared in the *New York Times* and numerous national travel magazines. She lives in Miami where she teaches tourism and geography at Miami-Dade Community College.

Jim Haskins and Joann Biondi are also co-authors of the *Hippocrene USA Guide to The Black South*.

Hippocrene U.S.A. Guide to
BLACK NEW YORK

Joann Biondi & James Haskins

HIPPOCRENE BOOKS
New York

Acknowledgments

The authors are grateful to Ann Kalkhoff, Kathy Benson, Jeanne DeQuine, and Martha Ellen Zenfell for their assistance.

For information, address
HIPPOCRENE BOOKS, INC.
171 Madison Avenue
New York, NY 10016

Library of Congress Cataloging-in-Publication Data
Biondi, Joann.
    Hippocrene U.S.A. guide to Black New York / Joann Biondi & James
Haskins.
        p. cm.
    Includes bibliographical references and index.
    ISBN 0-7818-0172-9
    1. Afro-Americans –New York (N.Y.) –History.   2. Historic sites –
New York (N.Y.) –Guidebooks.   3. New York (N.Y.) –Guidebooks.
I. Haskins, James, 1941- .   II. Title.   III. Title: Black New York.
F128.9.N3B5   1994
974.7'100496073–dc20   93-46137
                                                                CIP

Printed in the United States of America.

To Lynn Shreve

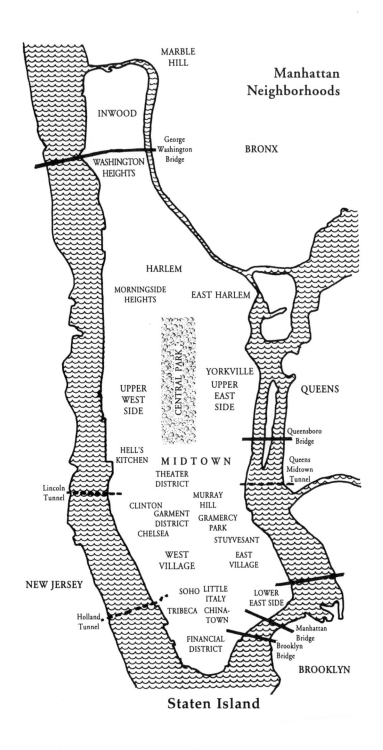

Manhattan
Neighborhoods

MARBLE
HILL

INWOOD

BRONX

George
Washington
Bridge

WASHINGTON
HEIGHTS

HARLEM

MORNINGSIDE
HEIGHTS

EAST HARLEM

CENTRAL PARK

YORKVILLE
UPPER
EAST
SIDE

QUEENS

UPPER
WEST
SIDE

Queensboro
Bridge

HELL'S
KITCHEN

MIDTOWN

Queens
Midtown
Tunnel

THEATER
DISTRICT

Lincoln
Tunnel

MURRAY
HILL

CLINTON
GARMENT
DISTRICT
CHELSEA

GRAMERCY
PARK

STUYVESANT

WEST
VILLAGE

EAST
VILLAGE

NEW JERSEY

SOHO

LITTLE
ITALY

LOWER
EAST SIDE

Holland
Tunnel

TRIBECA

CHINA-
TOWN

Manhattan
Bridge

FINANCIAL
DISTRICT

Brooklyn
Bridge

BROOKLYN

Staten Island

Contents

New York is a place where the rich walk, the poor drive Cadillacs, and beggars die of malnutrition with thousands of dollars hidden in their mattresses.

–Duke Ellington

Foreword

*F*rom ancient slave burial grounds hidden deep beneath modern buildings, to the soulful sounds of rhythm and blues that pulsate from the Apollo Theater, New York City is rich in African-American history. Scattered throughout the five boroughs are hundreds of sites that reveal the contributions African-Americans have made to the city, and the country. And fortunately, the city's African-American community has made keeping their culture alive a top priority. In the past few years, many people have been involved in preserving historic sites so that they don't disappear from the landscape and become lost forever.

Recent travel trends have shown that throughout the United States many sites of African-American significance are experiencing record numbers of visitors. More and more Americans, and travelers from abroad, are seeking out these spots because they are full of authenticity and a spirited sense of place. Similar to the growth in interest in Native American Indian reservations and other ethnic enclaves, the interest in African-American culture is tied to the desire to get in touch with the country's roots and explore its varied textures.

New York City is very much a part of this travel trend. Along with being home to over 17,000 restaurants, 3,500 churches, 1,500 parks, 700 landmark buildings, 400 art galleries, 200 theaters, 150 museums and 100 nightclubs, New York City is also home to the largest

BLACK NEW YORK

African-American community in the United States—almost 2 million people. And many of the 25 million tourists who visit the city each year are becoming aware of the cultural and historical landmarks of African-American significance within the city's limits.

The purpose of this book is to shed light on these landmarks, bring them to the forefront where they belong, and make finding them an easy and enjoyable task. The compilation of over 300 entries in this book includes historic sites, churches, theaters, museums, art galleries, restaurants, jazz joints, radio programs, record shops, schools, neighborhoods, dance companies, festivals, parks, and cemeteries—the essence of New York City's black communities. Some of the sites are well known and have already left their mark in American history books—like the Audubon Ballroom in Harlem where Malcolm X was slain, and the legendary Swing Street in midtown Manhattan. Others are more obscure—like the Plymouth Congregational Church in Brooklyn that once served as a stop on the Underground Railroad, or the grave of Scott Joplin, the great ragtime composer, in Astoria, Queens. A few of them are in hard-to-find nooks and crannies, others sit smack in the middle of bustling downtown. As a collection, they represent a bittersweet testimony to triumph over adversity, and a celebration of the unconquerable African-American spirit.

The book is divided into seven chapters, one for each of the five boroughs, one dedicated exclusively to Harlem, and a final chapter that lists helpful information and tour operators that specialize in African-American itineraries. Each chapter includes a brief introduction to the history of blacks in that area, followed by a series of listings arranged alphabetically. When applicable, hours of operation, addresses, and phone numbers have been included. Although not individually noted, many of the sites are closed during federal holidays. Since operating hours often change with time, phoning ahead is suggested.

For the curious tourist who feels the spiritual pull of the road-less-traveled, this book will serve as a guide to some of New York City's most overlooked landmarks. It is a journey into the sites, sounds, and tastes of the city's African-American legacy. Welcome to Historic Black New York!

The History of African-Americans in New York City

African-Americans have been a part of New York City for over 350 years, since it beginnings as the Dutch town of New Amsterdam in the colony of New Netherland. The first eleven slaves arrived in 1626, imported from the West Indies by the Dutch West India Company, the corporation which operated the colony under royal charter.

Rather than being owned by individuals, these slaves were designated as the "Company's People." They worked for the company laying the stones on the first paved street (Broad, subsequently named Stone), building Fort Amsterdam, and cultivating gardens and farms. Housed, fed and clothed by their employer, they were not chattel slaves; their labor was owned, but not their persons. They were allowed to own businesses and engage in other commercial pursuits. Their marriages and adoptions of children were recorded in legal records, and their children were granted an education. They also had the right to sue whites in court, and attend services at the Dutch Reformed church.

In 1644, these first eleven slaves were manumitted and given land grants to farmland about a mile north of the limits of the town proper (in present-day Greenwich Village). Thus began the history of black land ownership in North America. By the time of the British takeover, more than twenty farms were owned by free blacks.

But life became more restricted for the approximately 700 African-Americans in New York after the British assumed control of the Dutch colony in 1664. Gradually, the British implemented a variety of discriminatory regulations against the blacks. Slave marriages were no longer considered legal and slave children were no longer given an education. African-Americans, slave and free, were consigned to special galleries in the churches and were banned from burial in white churchyards, which resulted in the establishment of the Negroes Burial Ground outside the city limits. And in 1712, the titles of the land owned by freed African-Americans were rescinded by the British.

By the early 1700s, the number of African-Americans in New York had grown from the original eleven to more than 6,000. Eventually, many of them began to resent the harsh treatment they received from the British, and in 1712 New York experienced its first slave rebellion. A group of slaves and Native Indians set a fire in the center of town and then attacked the white inhabitants who tried to put out the flames. Behind the rebellion was the slaves' wish "to revenge themselves for some hard usage from their masters," according to the report from the governor to the British crown. Quickly rounded up from the nearby forests, some rebels committed suicide and twenty-one were executed, including two Indians.

A second suspected slave revolt occurred in 1714 when a series of mysterious fires cast the entire black population under suspicion. Remembering the bloody incident of 1712, city magistrates offered rewards for information leading to the arrest of guilty persons. The resulting spate of confessions and arrests was reminiscent of the witch trials in Salem, Massachusetts. By the time the so-called "Negro Plot" was over, an Irish indentured servant named Mary Burton had implicated not only her employers at an interracial tavern where the "Negro Plot" was supposedly organized, but also a great number of New York blacks. Hundreds of blacks were rounded up for questioning, and the city's small and ostracized Catholic population had also come under suspicion. By the time it was all over, 18 blacks had been hanged, 13 burned alive, and more than 70 deported to Africa. The tavern owners, a Catholic priest, and the Irish mistress of one of the black suspects were also executed.

By the time of the American Revolution, the attitude of some white New Yorkers toward the African-American population had become more liberal. Alexander Hamilton and John Jay lobbied for African-American enlistment in the colonial fighting forces, and many black New Yorkers fought in the Battle of Harlem Heights near what is now Columbia University.

Following the Revolution, the ideas of freedom percolated down to include freedom for African-American slaves. In 1781, Hamilton and Jay were instrumental in the founding of the New York Manumission Society as secretary and president, respectively. The aim of the society was the freedom of all blacks held in bondage and the education of their children. The Manumission Society founded the first African Free School in 1786, with 40 pupils of both sexes.

There were serious questions in the minds of many white New Yorkers about how to accommodate the city's would-be African-American citizens, however. In 1817, the American Colonization Society was established, its purpose being to send African-Americans to the American colony of Liberia in Africa. New York City's branch of the society was among the most active. It was strongly backed by the city's Protestant ministers, some of whom disciplined black ministers for opposing the plan.

In the meantime, free black New Yorkers had been taking steps to establish their own institutions. In 1795, Peter Williams and Richard Varick, tired of the discrimination blacks suffered at the white John Street Methodist Church, broke away from the congregation and began to hold separate meetings. In 1800, they erected their own church which later became known as the African Methodist Episcopal Zion Church. Other Protestant denominations soon had separate black congregations in New York, and in 1808

Abyssinian Baptist Church came into being. In 1820, Peter Williams, who had left the Methodist Church, became the first African-American ordained in the Episcopal Church and later became rector of St. Philips' Protestant Episcopal Church. The following year, the Reverend Samuel E. Cornish became the first pastor of the new Negro Presbyterian Church. Not only did these various churches form the basis for a new black community in lower Manhattan known as Little Africa, but they also provided African-Americans once again the opportunity to be buried in their sacred churchyards rather than in the Negroes Burial Ground.

The African Grove Theater was established on Bleecker Street and its first performance recorded in 1821. Another black theater was known to have existed in 1824 on Marion Street near Houston Street. In 1827, John B. Russwurm, who the year before had been the first African-American to graduate from Bowdoin College in Brunswick, Maine, along with the Reverend Samuel Cornish founded Freedom's Journal, the country's first black newspaper.

That same year, New York State officially abolished slavery, an edict that affected some 16,000 blacks, slave and free, in New York and Brooklyn. Blacks in New York rejoiced. So did the black oyster fishermen who plied the coast northward from Maryland and Delaware. On the shore of Staten Island, in a neighborhood called Sandy Ground, there was already a small community of black oyster fishermen; following emancipation in New York, that community was augmented by the oystermen from Maryland and Delaware. By 1850, the community had built Roseville African Methodist Episcopal Zion Church and established Sandy Ground as a vibrant African-American community. Other black communities also sprouted, among them Weeksville in Brooklyn.

Whites, especially newly arrived immigrants, had a different view of emancipation in the state. Almost as soon as the emancipation law was passed, groups of enraged whites, determined that blacks "keep their place" regardless of the law, assaulted blacks at whim. The number of such assaults grew so alarming that in 1829 city authorities closed all places where blacks were known to congregate because of the danger of civil disturbances. These places included all existing black theaters.

A great number of these whites were unskilled laborers, many of them Irish immigrants. They resented the competition for jobs by the newly freed slaves, and when these blacks moved into their neighborhoods, the tensions between the two groups became even more volatile.

The Five Points District, in the lower Manhattan area bounded by Park, Baxter and Worth Streets, was an Irish immigrant neighborhood before emancipation. Forced to seek their own lodgings once they were no longer housed in the homes of their former masters, the freed slaves could afford little more than the crowded squalor Five Points had to offer. More than 1,000 blacks and Irish lived in a single building, the Old Brewery. A run-down, five-story building, the Old Brewery held the infamous reputation as the site of at least one murder every night for more than 15 years.

The small, black middle-class resented the fact that the Irish immigrants, looked down upon by the more established white population, were granted rights denied to blacks. Elizabeth Jennings, a black New York City school teacher whose family were pillars in the community, expressed this resentment when she was put off a whites-only street car on her way to church one Sunday morning in 1854. In a huff, Jennings reportedly told the conductor that she was a respectable person, born and raised in New York, and asked him where he had been born. The driver, an Irish immigrant, was outraged by her remarks and felt that she was showing the very anti-Irish bias that was typical of New York blacks. Jennings, in retaliation, brought suit against the Third Avenue Railway Company. Represented by the firm of Culver-Parker, Jennings made her case that the railway company had discriminated against her merely on the basis of her race. She won in court, and as a result of her action all New York City street cars were desegregated.

Other members of New York's small black middle-class made

their mark in the mid-1800s, although in a largely anonymous way. They took part in the network, known as the Underground Railroad, that helped thousands of slaves find their way to a better life in the North. New York City's black churches were active in this area, as were many individual African-American citizens. David Ruggles, a freed man from Massachusetts, was one of the best-known New York City agents in the anti-slavery cause. He was director of the New York Committee of Vigilance, which sought to combat the seizure of New York blacks by Southern slave holders and their agents. Ruggles also published anti-slavery materials which no doubt explained the mysterious fire that burned his books and library in 1835 and was an important agent on the Underground Railroad. Another notable was Henry Highland Garnet, who had run away with his family from New Market, Maryland. Pastor for more than 40 years of Shiloh Presbyterian Church in New York City, Garnet attended the National Convention of Negro Citizens in Buffalo, New York, in 1843, and there implored all slaves to arise: "Strike for your lives and liberties. Now is the day and the hour. Let every slave throughout the land do this, and the days of slavery are numbered."

Within 15 years, the nation was at war over the issue of slavery. In the early days of the war, which was expected to last only a short time, both the North and the South had scores of willing volunteers, including, in both regions, many African-Americans who were denied the opportunity to serve. In New York City, a group of black men rented a hall and began drill practice in case they were called to serve. But the police stopped them, warning that there was no way to protect them from mob assault by the "lower classes" of the city, namely the Irish immigrants. That warning proved to be prophetic.

After two years of fighting, new volunteers were few, necessitating both sides to institute a draft. Written into the draft act on both sides was a way out for wealthy citizens, who could buy their exemptions for comparatively large sums of money.

In the North, the great majority who could not afford to buy their way out of the draft were subject to a lottery. The New York City lottery began on Saturday, July 11, 1863. By Monday morning, July 13, the Draft Riots were raging across the city as mobs, primarily of Irish immigrants, rebelled. First aimed at federal authorities and city police, the attacks soon concentrated on the city's black population, for the rioters saw slavery and blacks as the main reason for the war and the resultant Draft Law. In the course of four days, angry mobs ran rampant, attacking any blacks who happened to be in their way and burning the Colored Orphan Asylum at 43rd Street and Fifth Avenue.

Within a few months, the federal government had changed its mind about accepting black enlistments. In 1864 the Twentieth Regiment United States Colored Troops marched down Broadway to great fanfare. By the end of the war, more than 800 black New Yorkers had given their lives in the Union cause.

After the war was over, according to Roi Ottley and William J. Weatherby in their seminal 1967 work The Negro in New York, "Negroes of the North dropped into a place of insignificance nationally... a position from which they did not emerge to any appreciable degree until the United States entered the World War. The arena for the Negro had shifted from the North to the South."

The passage of the Thirteenth, Fourteenth, and Fifteenth Amendments, which ended slavery, gave blacks the rights of citizenship and the right to vote, also gave Northern blacks a sense of complacency. The various anti-slavery organizations died for lack of a cause and the black newspapers ceased publication.

In New York, there was some basis for this sense of security. By 1870 black New Yorkers constituted a sizable population some 60,000 people. William Marcy "Boss" Tweed sought to take advantage of these numbers and the new suffrage guarantees by supporting a variety of gambling clubs and dance halls run by blacks in exchange for votes. Working class blacks had a brief opportunity to join in the burgeoning national union movement.

Post-war prosperity elevated some members of the black middle class to the first black upper class in New York. African-American inventors had opportunities as never before to enjoy credit for their discoveries: Granville T. Woods, a native of Ohio, invented the "third-rail" system that enabled electricity to replace steam on elevated railways. In New York City, after the installation of Woods' system, innocent blacks were sometimes attacked because Woods' invention had put a lot of white railway employees out of work. Woods relocated to New York in 1880, and soon after invented a telegraph system which made communication between moving trains possible.

After the Civil War, black entertainers were finally free to reclaim the minstrel-show format that had been popularized by whites in black-face during the years when blacks were unable to move freely around the country. By this time, the black-face minstrel format was so firmly entrenched that even black entertainers had to perform in black-face. But black entertainers brought new life to the minstrel shows and helped lay the foundation for the American musical. A number of musicals written and performed by blacks opened in New York in the late 1890s, and several black entertainers, including the teams of Williams and Walker and Cole and Johnson, enjoyed considerable success.

That success made them special targets in the summer of 1900, when a fight between a white man and a black man at the corner of Eighth Avenue and Forty-first Street resulted in the death of the white man and a rampage by white mobs against blacks. "Get Cole and Johnson! Get Williams and Walker!" the mobs shouted, referring to the only blacks they knew by name. They menacingly congregated outside the clubs and theaters where those entertainers were appearing, and the police did nothing to quell their anger. The black entertainers escaped by themselves.

By the early 1900s, black athletes had also come to the forefront in New York City. The Cuban Giants, who were loved for their lightning-quick skills at baseball, were popular. Several black boxers made names for themselves in New York, although most were from other parts of the country or the world. Unlike the black baseball players, the black boxers were able to engage in open competition with white opponents. Nova Scotia native George Dixon and West Indian Joe Wolcott made their marks in New York by beating white opponents. Jack Johnson, who defeated Jim Jeffries in Reno, Nevada, in July of 1910, was not a New Yorker, but his victory over "the great white hope" for the heavyweight championship caused white mobs in New York City to swarm throughout the black neighborhoods.

Beginning around 1900, blacks started moving into the West Sixties creating a neighborhood that known as San Juan Hill, a reference to the recent Spanish-American War and the numerous fights that occurred in the neighborhood between the blacks and the Irish immigrants. The assault on the blacks who lived in this neighborhood by white mobs after the Johnson victory stimulated the northward move by blacks to Harlem.

In the early 1900s, Harlem was considered one of the finest residential sections in New York. A place of wide, tree-lined boulevards and new brownstone apartment houses, it had been planned as a white suburb of downtown. But over-speculation in real estate and delays in the completion of the elevated railway service to the area opened the way for black residents who were willing to pay sky-high rents in order to escape the racial turmoil of areas such as San Juan Hill. Once the major black institutions, such as Abyssinian Baptist Church, had moved to Harlem, it fast became the legendary Capital of Black America.

Meanwhile, a small but important reform movement had begun. Shocked by race riots in 1903 in Abraham Lincoln's birthplace, Springfield, Illinois, some white liberals sought to revive the spirit of the abolitionist movement. They joined with African-Americans such as W.E.B. DuBois, a black intellectual and Harvard graduate who had formed a national organization called the Niagra Movement, whose purpose, among others, was "the abolition of all caste distinctions based on color or race."

In 1909, the National Association for the Advancement of Colored People was formed in New York City by an interracial group. DuBois founded and was the first editor of its periodical, The Crisis. The following year, another interracial organization, the National Urban League, was created.

Both organizations urged African-American support of the United States cause in World War I, and thousands of New York City blacks served in that war. The 369th Regiment out of New York City, although under white command, was the first black unit to be sent to the front lines in Europe and the first to distinguish itself in combat. Attached to a French unit, the 369th was awarded France's highest military honor, the Croix de Guerre, for gallantry under fire. The band attached to the 369th Regiment was led by James Reese Europe, who, with other black bandmasters, brought the sizzling sounds of jazz to the European continent.

The drum major in Europe's band was Noble Sissle, who after the war joined with Eubie Blake to form an entertainment team. They got together with another duo, Flournoy Miller and Aubrey Lyles, and produced "Shuffle Along," the first black musical on Broadway, which opened in 1919.

"Shuffle Along" was evidence of, as well as stimulus to, a new black consciousness that found expression in a variety of forums, among them the black nationalism of Jamaican-born Marcus Garvey's United Negro Improvement Association and Back-to-Africa Movement. Garvey's talent for showmanship brought his movement more attention than its numbers warranted, but his philosophy touched a chord in the hearts of many African-American New Yorkers who were tired of their second-class status.

More popular were the theories of Washington-born Alain Locke, Harvard Phi Beta Kappa and the first black Rhodes Scholar, who advanced the notion of the "New Negro" in the post-war era. New York, and Harlem in particular, were becoming a mecca for black people, and the confluence of talent produced the great intellectual and artistic flowering that came to be called the Harlem Renaissance. Writers like Locke, Langston Hughes, and Zora Neale Hurston, and artists such as Romare Bearden, Hale Woodruff, and Augusta Savage found a new, white audience for their work and the elbow-rubbing between uptown black artists and the downtown white intelligensia was unprecedented.

White interest in Harlem blossomed and was fertilized by Prohibition, when mob-run, whites-only nightclubs offered not only bootleg liquor but a taste of the exotic in entertainment. Musicians and singers such as Duke Ellington, Louis Armstrong, Lena Horne, and Ethel Waters enjoyed a popularity unheard of for African-American entertainers.

It was at this time that New York City's nickname, the Big Apple, became popular. Although some say the term may have first been used in race-track lingo, it was used by black jazz musicians who referred to gigs in smaller cities as playing "the branches" and the highly coveted bookings in New York as playing the Big Apple.

By the early 1930s, greater black in-migration from the South and the West Indies began to strain the available housing in Harlem. Mob wars made the nighttime streets of Harlem less attractive to white revelers, and the repeal of Prohibition along with the onset of the Great Depression effectively ended the Harlem Renaissance. Blacks, "last hired and first fired," suffered disproportionately during the Depression. Resentment against white businesses in Harlem that refused to hire black workers boiled over in March 1935 after a young Puerto Rican boy, caught stealing a knife at a West 135th Street Kress five-and-dime, was rumored to have been beaten by the store's white employees. Harlemites rioted, destroying tens of thousands of dollars worth of white-owned stores and merchandise.

Adam Clayton Powell, Jr., the young pastor of Abyssinian Baptist Church, first came to prominence at this time. He organized protests against white-owned stores that refused to hire blacks, and set forth a black boycott against utility and bus companies to force them to hire blacks.

The onset of World War II in Europe lifted Harlem out of the Depression along with the rest of the country. Black New Yorkers rallied to the cause and distinguished themselves in air and ground combat, when given the opportunity. New York City-based A. Philip Randolph, who had founded the Brotherhood of Sleeping Car Porters, the first black union, and his aide, Bayard Rustin, pressed President Truman to desegregate the armed forces. Truman finally issued the order in 1948, and the next time the United States went to war, in Korea, blacks and whites fought together.

The National Association for the Advancement of Colored People had for decades waged a drive in the courts against school desegregation. Thurgood Marshall, who headed up the separate legal branch of the organization in New York, spearheaded the legal campaign that led to the landmark Supreme Court decision in Brown v. Board of Education that declared separate but equal education unconstitutional.

As in the post-Civil War era, the arena for the civil rights struggle was primarily the South, but New York City blacks made their mark. Stokely Carmichael, who was born in Trinidad but raised in New York and educated at the Bronx High School of Science, participated in the Student Nonviolent Coordinating Committee's Mississippi Freedom Summer in 1964, and two years later became the executive director of the SNCC. But many African-Americans in New York City looked askance at the philosophies of nonviolent protest espoused by the founders of the SNCC and Martin Luther King, Jr. Like most other Northern urban blacks, they were attracted instead to the nationalism of the charismatic Malcolm X.

Malcolm X almost single-handedly brought the Chicago-based Nation of Islam to national prominence. After Elijah Muhammad, leader of the movement called the Black Muslims, appointed Malcolm X minister of the new Temple Number Seven in Harlem, Malcolm X took advantage of his location in the media capital of the world. Articulate and provocative, he personally accounted for a substantial number of converts to the Nation of Islam. His role as a media star, and his tendency to make political statements against the wishes of Elijah Muhammad, led eventually to his being "silenced" as a spokesman for the Nation, and to his assassination by Muslims at Harlem's Audubon Ballroom in 1965.

Although it has had its brash moments, black political activity in New York City has historically been conservative. New York renegades, like the Reverend Al Sharpton, often get more media attention than they do black voter support. Never truly constituting a substantial voting bloc, black New Yorkers have seen unwavering Democratic Party loyalists win the few major offices to be occupied by blacks in America. Manhattan Borough Presidents Hulan Jack in the 1950s and Percy Sutton in the 1970s were Democratic Party stalwarts. Former Mayor David Dinkens, a longtime Democratic loyalist who had served as City Clerk and Manhattan Borough President before moving into Gracie Mansion in 1989, is one of the few who have triumphed at coalition-building. His term as the first African-American mayor of New York City proved that blacks are very much a part of New York history. A history that has come a long way since the first eleven slaves arrived in 1626.

Chapter 1

Manhattan

*F*or many of the 1.5 million people who live there, Manhattan is the greatest place on earth, the center of the universe, a distinct state of mind. Only thirteen miles long and two miles wide, it is an island with no rival. Beneath its jagged skyline, Manhattan is a combination of explosive vitality and extreme nonchalance. It is a push-and-shove kind of place where day-to-day life is a theatrical performance, and derelicts have turned panhandling into an art form. Its kaleidoscope of characters include people of many races, cultures, and nationalities who sometimes blend and other times collide. On this one small island you can find rap dancers monopolizing a corner, street vendors selling Kente cloth hats, cool jazz in the Village, Jelly's Last Jam on Broadway, and Ethiopian injeri bread baked fresh to order.

For most travelers who visit New York, New York means Manhattan, and Manhattan is brimming with African-American history. In the beginning, when the Dutch settlers first landed on the island in the early 1600s, they brought with them shiploads of African slaves by way of Brazil and the Caribbean. These African slaves cleared the land, tended the cattle, and built forts to defend the territory then known as New Amsterdam. A few decades later, when the British raised the Union Jack over Fort Amsterdam and renamed the town New York, they too brought with them a passel of African

slaves, and established a bustling slave market along the East River
near what is now Wall Street.

In the centuries that followed, the descendants of the African
slaves continued to contribute to the development of Manhattan,
and managed to carve out a life of their own while coping with the
harsh prejudices and unjust circumstances that restrained their
chances for advancement. They established their own neighborhoods such as Five Points and San Juan Hill; and built their own
schools, churches, cemeteries, orphanages, grocery stores, barber
shops, restaurants, theaters, and music clubs. They helped their
distant cousins escape from the South by creating a Manhattan
network for the Underground Railroad. They rebelled against re-
pression and fought for civil rights.

Today, African-Americans are very much a part of mainstream
Manhattan. Their art work hangs in the finest museums, their music
is performed at Carnegie Hall, and bold statues of them grace the
lawns of Central Park. African-Americans power-lunch on Wall
Street, display their designer creations in the Fashion District,
anchor the evening news, perform ballet on stage, shop at Tiffany's,
and have an influential voice in their borough's politics.

Within the canyons of concrete and glass, Manhattan is a treas-
ure-trove of African-American history. With just a little bit of effort,
a traveler can find the old Negroes Burial Ground, areas where slave
uprisings took place, the site of the African Grove Theater, Swing
Street, Scott Joplin's boarding house, and the apartment building
where blues singer Billie Holiday spent the last year of her life. They
can also find many other reminders of the contributions African-
Americans have made to Manhattan.

HISTORIC SITES AND CULTURAL CENTERS

African-American Bookstore Historic Site—67 Lispenard St., lower Manhattan. At this site during the late 1700s, famed black abolitionist David Ruggles established a bookstore and reading room for African-Americans who were not permitted to use the city's libraries.

African-American Institute—833 United Nations Plaza, 47th Street and 1st Avenue, Manhattan. (212) 949-5666. Hours: Mon.-Fri. 9a.m.-5p.m., Sat. 11a.m.-5p.m. Located across the street from the United Nations, the African-American Institute is a private organization devoted to development in Africa and strengthening the understanding Americans have of the continent. The institute's exhibit space at U.N. Plaza is not large, but it does feature three fine quality exhibits a year. Drawn from private museums and collections, the exhibits are based on traditional and contemporary African arts and crafts from throughout the continent, and include embroidered costumes, wooden sculptures, batiks, masks, ancient terra cottas, fertility dolls, and art for children.

African Burial Ground and the Commons Historic District—Broadway, between Reade and Duane Streets, Manhattan. During the 1700s, this area near modern-day City Hall was a desolate spot situated outside the city limits known as the Negroes Burial Ground. At the time, blacks were not allowed to join the city's churches, so church burial grounds within the city limits were not open to them.

In 1991, as a $276 million, 42-story federal office tower was being built on the site, construction workers accidentally unearthed the first of more than 400 bodies found 20 feet below the ground. Historians estimate that the cemetery once covered nearly six acres, and held the remains of more than 20,000 African-Americans who lived and died in Manhattan. Many are thought to have been first generation African-Americans, both free and enslaved blacks.

Contained in plain wooden coffins, the skeletal remains were studied by a team of archeologists and a close examination revealed: infants buried in their mothers' arms, coins placed on some of the skeletons' eyes and hands, and buttons from a British officer's uniform worn by a high-ranking black during the Revolutionary

War. The area adjacent to the burial ground, during the 18th century, was a commons used for public displays ranging from hangings to the first reading of the Declaration of Independence in the city. In addition to the skeletal remains, more than 1.5 million artifacts were recovered from the commons area.

Under pressure from the African-American community and historic preservationists, members of Congress along with Mayor Dinkens forced the building's owner to change its design, thereby eliminating a pavilion that would have been built above the site of most of the graves, though still allowing the building to be constructed. In 1993, the city's Landmarks Preservation Commission declared the site an historic landmark and restricted any further disruption of the graves. The site was named the African Burial Ground and the Commons Historic District, and plans are being considered to construct a museum in the area devoted to the colonial-era history of blacks.

African Free School No. 1 Historic Site—137 Mulberry St., in the Little Italy neighborhood of lower Manhattan. During the mid-1800s, this was the site of the African Free School No. 1, one of the few places where poor black children could get an education in Manhattan. By 1830, six such schools were operating in lower Manhattan.

African Grove Theater Historic Site—At the corner of Mercer and Bleecker Streets in Greenwich Village, Manhattan. Owned and operated by African-Americans from 1820 to 1830, the African Grove Theater offered live dramatic productions and operas to the black community. According to an advertisement about the theater from the time, "Neither time nor expense had been spared rendering this entertainment agreeable to ladies and gentlemen of color." The theater was eventually forced to close by city officials who thought that it might annoy the whites who lived in the neighborhood.

Alvin Ailey American Dance Center—11 W. 61st St., Manhattan. (212) 767-0940. The official dance school of the revered company where modern, jazz, and ballet classes are offered. Single class sessions and intensive summer workshops are available.

American Craft Museum—40 W. 53rd St., Manhattan. (212) 956-3535. Hours: Tues. 10a.m-8p.m., Wed.-Sun. 10a.m.-5p.m. An intimate and folksy museum with three major exhibits each year dedicated to a variety of American crafts such as sweet grass baskets, quilts, pottery, clothing, musical instruments, and cookware. Exhibits often include works by African-Americans.

American Museum of Natural History—Central Park West and 79th Street, Manhattan. (212) 769-5100. Hours: Sun., Mon., Tues., Thur. 10a.m.-5:45p.m.; Wed., Fri., Sat. 10a.m.-9p.m. Occupying four city blocks, the American Museum of Natural History holds some of the finest zoology, anthropology and natural science exhibits in the world. Included are the Akeley Memorial Hall of African Mammals; the Man in Africa exhibit which explains the diversity of cultures on the continent; exhibits focusing on tribal religions and African musical instruments such as drums, harps, lutes, and clapping sticks.

Baxter Street Historic Site—42 Baxter Street, now the Criminal Courts Building in lower Manhattan. This was once the site of the first clubhouse of the New York African Society for Mutual Relief. Despite the harsh penalties imposed on blacks who got caught meeting together, members of the society assembled here in the early 1800s. They offered each other moral support and intellectual stimulation, and worked to help needy black families in the fight against discrimination. Several of the clubhouse members played prominent roles in the first National Convention of Colored People of the United States in 1831 in Philadelphia.

Billie Holiday's Last New York City Residence—26 W. 86th Street, Manhattan. The great blues singer Billie Holiday spent the last year of her life here in this apartment, sad, lonely and in poor health. With her career in a slump, and her alcoholism and drug addiction taking their toll on her spirit, Holiday languished in this apartment for days at a time without seeing or talking to anyone.

In May of 1959 she collapsed into a coma and was rushed to a hospital. A few days later the police searched her hospital room and allegedly found a small amount of heroine. Holiday's books, radios and personal belongings were confiscated by the police, and she was finger-printed while in her hospital bed. About a month later, on July 17, she died.

Birdland Historic Site—1678 Broadway, Manhattan. During the 1950s, the basement of this midtown building housed Birdland, one of New York's most popular jazz and bebop clubs. Opened in 1949 by Charlie "Yardbird" Parker, for whom the club was named, Birdland was a lively place with a dance floor, a milk bar for non-drinkers, bleachers for those who just wanted to watch, and a midget announcer named Pee Wee Marquette.

It was at Birdland that Charlie Parker tried to commit suicide one night by drinking a bottle of iodine, and on another night had a boisterous fight with a band member causing Charles Mingus, who also played in the band, to apologize to the audience. Parker was eventually banned from his own club.

It was also at Birdland, in 1959, that Miles Davis was badly beaten by two policemen as he took a breather outside between sets. Davis was charged with disorderly conduct, but after an outpouring of public protest, the charges were dropped. Following the incident, Davis' political stance took on a more militant character.

Black Bohemia Historic Site—W. 53rd Street and surrounding area, Manhattan. During the 1890s, this mid-Manhattan neighborhood was known as Black Bohemia. Many blacks lived in the area and established it as a center for black theater, music and sports professionals.

Black Filmmakers Foundation—80 8th Ave., suite 1704, Manhattan. (212) 941-3944. The largest distributor of independent black films and videos in the country, the BFF also serves as a research center for aspiring young filmmakers by offering workshops, lectures and access to its large video library.

Blue Room Historic Site—700 8th Ave., at 44th Street, Manhattan. Now the Milford Plaza, this old brick building was once the Lincoln Hotel, home of the famous Blue Room nightclub. In 1938, Billie Holiday performed here but she was not allowed to enter through the front door. Describing her bafflement over the club's segregation policy, Holiday told a reporter for the *Amsterdam News*, "It's funny, we were really a big hit all over the South and never ran into the color question until we opened at the Lincoln Hotel here in New York City. I was never allowed to visit the bar or the dining room. Not only was I made to enter and leave the hotel through the kitchen, but I had to remain alone in a little dark room all evening until I was called." During the 1940s, Count Bassie performed at the Blue Room.

Bricktop's Residence—155 W. 68th St., The Dorchester, Manhattan. Born Ada Beatrice Queen Victoria Louise Virginia Smith in Alderson, West Virginia, Bricktop—or Bricky as her cafe-society friends called her—was one of the most famous nightclub owners and impresarios in the world from the 1920s through the 1960s.

Her clubs were located in the chic districts of France, Italy and Mexico; and her list of friends and confidants included Josephine Baker, Duke Ellington, Noel Coward, Ernest Hemingway, Tallulah Bankhead, F. Scott Fitzgerald, Frank Sinatra, Elizabeth Taylor, and Richard Burton. T.S. Elliot put her in a poem, Cole Porter asked her to give dance lessons at his parties, and the Duke of Windsor spent many mornings next to the piano in her clubs. In 1972, after a lifetime of jet-setting around the world, Bricktop settled into this apartment building where many of her friends came to visit. She died in 1984 and is buried in Woodlawn Cemetery in the Bronx.

Buckley's Ethiopian Opera House Historic Site—539 Broadway in Greenwich Village, Manhattan. During the mid-1800s, Buckley's was an extremely popular theater where white New York actors performed in blackface. Eddie Leonard, one of the greatest blackface performers of all time, performed here regularly. Few people knew that Leonard was actually a black from Virginia.

Cafe Society Historic Site—2 Sheridan Sq., near W. 4th Street, lower Manhattan. Cafe Society in the 1940s was one of the first fully integrated nightclubs in the downtown area. Whites and blacks were allowed to sit, dance and mingle together without any heads turning to stare. Billie Holiday performed here as did Sarah Vaughan, Lena Horne, Art Tatem, and Joe Turner. Cafe Society closed in 1950.

Caribbean Cultural Center—408 W. 58th St., Manhattan. (212) 307-7420. Hours vary. This social center is dedicated to joining all cultures from Africa with a varied program of music, art, religion, lectures, and conferences.

Carnegie Hall—W. 57th Street and 7th Avenue, Manhattan. (212) 247-7800. New York's oldest and finest concert auditorium, Carnegie Hall has been the scene of many memorable African-American triumphs in music. History was made here in 1912 when James Reese Europe, America's first black bandleader, held New York's first jazz concert. With his 125 musicians, Europe received rave reviews and went on to conduct several more jazz concerts at Carnegie Hall.

In 1928, jazz pianists Fats Waller and James P. Johnson played a tribute concert to W.C. Handy at Carnegie Hall, and in 1938 the auditorium hosted the historic "From Spirituals to Swing" concert in honor of Bessie Smith; it was the first major New York concert for an integrated audience. Also in 1938, Bennie Goodman gave a concert performance at Carnegie Hall that was followed by a popular recording of the event, and soon after became known as the "King of Swing." Duke Ellington performed his "Black, Brown, and Beige" in 1943, and Charlie Parker played Carnegie Hall in the late 1940s. Today, major jazz acts are an important part of the auditorium's concert lineup.

Castle Clinton—Battery Park, lower Manhattan. This reddish stone building was once a fort that served as a defense against the British in the War of 1812. Declared a national monument in 1950, Castle Clinton was the site in 1851 where an official city reception was held for Hungarian revolutionary leader Louis Kossuth. One of the delegations that met with Kossuth was a group of African-Americans who conveyed to Kossuth the sympathy New York blacks had for Hungarian peasants, and how much they hoped the Hungarians would attain their freedom.

Central Park—From 59th to 110th Streets and 5th Avenue to Central Park West, Manhattan. New York City's favorite playground, Central Park was designed by landscape architect Frederick Law Olmstead. Along with being a genius at landscape design, Olmstead was an ardent abolitionist who spent a great deal of time traveling through the South trying to convince slave owners that what they were doing was morally wrong and economically unsound. After he started work on Central Park, Olmstead temporarily put it aside in order to devote his time to the Union cause in the Civil War. After the war he worked with the Freedman's Bureau helping blacks adjust to their new conditions. He was also the author of the slave period classic essay "A Journey in the Seaboard Slave States."

Charles Mingus' Residence—5 Great Jones St., near Lafayette Street, Greenwich Village, Manhattan. During the mid-1960s, jazz musician Charles Mingus lived in a loft apartment here while playing engagements at the nearby Village Gate. In 1966, he was evicted for allegedly not paying his rent. The incident was portrayed in the Tom Reichman film *Mingus*.

Charlie Parker's Residence—151 Ave. B, near 10th Street, Greenwich Village, Manhattan. During the early 1950s, Charlie Parker lived in a comfortable apartment in this four-story building with his girlfriend, Chan, and their daughter, Kim. He moved here in 1951, a few years after his nervous breakdown due to drug addiction, and enjoyed several years as the premier jazz artist in New York playing with Erroll Garner's band, Dizzy Gillespie's band, and a series of his own groups that included Miles Davis and drummer Max Roach. Parker made his final appearance at Birdland in 1955, and died that same year of a heart attack.

Cinque Gallery—560 Broadway, Suite 504, Manhattan. (212) 966-3464. Hours: Tues.-Sat. 1-6p.m. Closed on Saturday during the summer months. For over 20 years, the Cinque Gallery has served as a fine viewing gallery for African-American art featuring both established and up-and-coming artists. The not-for-profit gallery hosts about six shows a year with emphasis on paintings, sculptures, ceramics, prints and photographs. It was established in 1969 by three of the most noted African-American artists in the country—Romare Bearden, Norman Lewis, and Ernest Critchlow.

City Hall— Chambers Street, near Broadway, Manhattan. (212) 566-5700. One of New York City's architectural jewels, City Hall was principally designed by black architect Joseph Francis Mangin. Officially opened in 1811, it is an elegant example of the Federal style.

Colored Orphan Asylum Historic Site—5th Avenue between 44th and 45th Streets in midtown Manhattan. During the mid-1800s, this was the site of the enormous Colored Orphan Asylum which housed hundreds of black children. Founded by two white women, the orphanage was burned to the ground in 1863 during the Civil War draft riots when angry white mobs broke into the orphanage shouting "Burn the niggers' nest!" The children were quickly whisked out a rear door and escaped unharmed, except for one little girl who hid under her bed, and was dragged out by the mob and beaten to death. For days later, the bloodbath continued, and blacks in the neighborhood were hunted down, hoisted onto lampposts, and set on fire.

Cooper-Hewitt Museum (Smithsonian Institution's National Museum of Design)—2 E. 91st St., at 5th Avenue, Manhattan. (212) 860-6868. Hours: Wed.-Sat. 10a.m.-5p.m., Tues. 10a.m.-

9p.m., Sun. noon-5p.m. The museum's 165,000 piece collection includes decorative art objects from Africa such as tie-dyed fabrics from the Ivory Coast, Zulu baskets, raffia cloth from Zaire, and an array of Kente cloth. The museum also offers lectures on African-American arts and crafts.

Cooper Union Foundation Building—Cooper Square at the intersection of 3rd Avenue and 7th Street in lower Manhattan. This historic building, constructed in 1859, served as a public forum before and during the Civil War. It was here that Abraham Lincoln made the speech that won him the Republican nomination for the presidency in 1860, and abolitionists Frederick Douglass and Wendell Phillips made frequent appearances.

David Ruggles Historic Homesite—36 Lispenard St., in lower Manhattan's TriBeCa neighborhood. David Ruggles was an African-American sailor who helped over 600 runaway slaves escape to freedom during the early and mid-1800s. He resided here when not traveling by land and sea to areas where he worked as a "conductor" on the Underground Railroad. For years, Ruggles was wanted by authorities who offered a reward for his head.

Duke Ellington Statue—Central Park, 5th Avenue near 110th Street, Manhattan. Commissioned for the park by the Duke Ellington Memorial Fund, this 20-foot high statue in honor of the great jazz musician was designed by Los Angeles artist Robert Graham.

Electric Lady Studios Historic Site—52 W. 8th St., near 6th Avenue, lower Manhattan. During the early 1970s, this four-story brownstone with a ground floor shaped like a guitar, housed rock guitarist Jimi Hendrix's recording studio. Hendrix created this studio in early 1970 and outfitted it with state-of-the-art instruments, beautiful art work, and carpet covered walls. He recorded over 600 hours of tapes here. Hendrix died on September 18, 1970, of a drug overdose, and the music he recorded here was posthumously released as albums.

Years before Hendrix took over this property, it was also tied to music and African-American history. During the 1960s it housed a music club called the Generation, where Hendrix and B.B. King performed together the night that Martin Luther King, Jr., was killed. Although the studio is long gone, a plaque that reads "Electric Lady" still hangs on the front door.

Elizabeth Jennings Historic Site—3rd Avenue, lower Manhattan. In 1854, while riding down 3rd Avenue in lower Manhattan, Elizabeth Jennings was thrown off a streetcar reserved for whites. Jennings, a school teacher and church organist, was the Rosa Parks of her day. With the support of the black community, she hired the law firm of Culver-Parker, known for its anti-slavery causes, to defend her case. Attorney Chester A. Arthur, the future president of the U.S., won the case for Jennings, and as a result of the suit, all New York City streetcars were desegregated.

Explorers Club—46 E. 70th St., Manhattan. (212) 628-8383. By appointment only. Founded in 1905, the Explorers Club is a private, non-profit organization composed of explorers and researchers. Its first African-American member was Matthew Henson, the explorer who accompanied Admiral Peary on his trips to the Arctic, and the man who actually planted the American flag at the North Pole. A more recent African-American member is Allen Counter, a researcher who wrote a book about Peary and Henson. The club offers lectures and educational programs.

Five Points District Historic Site—areas surrounding the State of New York Building on Centre Street in lower Manhattan. During the early 1800s, this district at the intersection of Park, Baxter and Worth Streets was the center of New York's African-American population, complete with schools, churches, homes and businesses. Most of the blacks lived in small basement apartments where several families crowded together in once space. Five Points, however, had a large number of unsavory characters and was a rough and poverty-stricken neighborhood. Blackbirders—gangs who kidnapped free, young blacks and later sold them as slaves in the South—roamed the streets. Mothers worried about allowing their children to go outside alone for fear that they would never return home again. During the Civil War draft riots in 1863, white gangs who dominated the area attacked many blacks and destroyed their properties.

One of the few whites who lived in Five Points was David Broderick. A stonecutter who went to California during the Gold Rush of 1849, Broderick was elected to the state's first Territorial Legislature and was an influential anti-slavery force in the decision that enabled California to enter the Union as a free state.

Fraunces Tavern and Museum—54 Pearl St., lower Manhattan. (212) 425-1778. Hours: Mon.-Fri. 10a.m.-4:45p.m., Sat. noon-4p.m. One of the oldest landmarks of Revolutionary days in New York City, the Fraunces Tavern during the late 1700s was owned by Samuel Fraunces, who historians believe was a black French West Indian. Known in New York as Black Sam, Fraunces established the tavern that was to become world famous.

It was at the Fraunces Tavern that the Liberty Boys plotted the Revolution, the New York Chamber of Commerce was organized, and General George Washington gave an emotional farewell address to his officers of the Continental Army in 1783. Black Sam's daughter, Phoebe, saved Washington's life by stopping him from eating food poisoned by one of his body guards. Following Washington's election as president, Samuel Fraunces was appointed steward of the presidential mansion which was then located in New York. When the U.S. capital was relocated to Philadelphia, Fraunces continued his duties there.

The tavern is still in operation and serves breakfast, lunch and dinner to the local Wall Street crowd. The museum is located on the tavern's second and third floors and houses rotating exhibits on the tavern's history and the Revolutionary War including a lock of George Washington's hair. The building is owned by the Sons of the Revolution and the organization still uses it for meetings.

George Gershwin's Residence—316 W. 103rd St., upper Manhattan. This small stone house is where George Gershwin lived from 1925 to 1931. Gershwin, the white composer who wrote the musical score for "Porgy and Bess," one of the most successful plays of the century, had an enormous influence on the New York music and theater scene. The home is marked with a plaque honoring George and his brother Ira who collaborated on many great works here.

Gramercy Park—Between 3rd Avenue and Park Avenue South, and E. 20th to 21st Streets in lower Manhattan. This beautifully land-scaped park surrounded by neat townhouses sits in the middle of one of Manhattan's most desirable neighborhoods. It was only a barren swamp when Peter Stuyvesant's widow sold it to one of her former slaves.

Great Negro Plot Historic Site—Broadway near Reade Street and City Hall, lower Manhattan. In 1714, this area then called "upper Manhattan," housed a gathering spot known as Hughson's Tavern. The tavern served as a secret meeting place where blacks, supposedly, conspired to take over the city in what was called "the Great Negro Plot." After several mysterious fires erupted throughout Manhattan, Mary Burton, an indentured servant and barmaid at Hughson's Tavern, told authorities that the plot was organized from the tavern. A city-wide investigation soon followed and concluded that a slave conspiracy was underway. Fearful of a slave uprising, New York authorities rounded up the suspects and 34 people were convicted. Thirteen black men were burned at the stake and 18 hanged; two white men, including tavern owner Hughson, were also hanged. Following the incident, more than 70 New York City blacks were forced to leave the country.

Hotel Roosevelt—Madison Avenue at 45th St., Manhattan. (212) 661-9600. Once the home base for bandleader Guy Lombardo, the Hotel Roosevelt was where the Benny Goodman Orchestra per-formed its first dancehall engagement. Unfortunately, the act didn't do very well. Patrons complained about the music and the waiters kept telling Goodman to play softer.

John Hammond's Residence—9 E. 91st St., Manhattan. Record producer and writer John Hammond grew up in this beautiful six-story mansion. Hammond was responsible for discovering and promoting many great African-American talents such as Billie Holiday, Count Bassie, Bessie Smith, and Aretha Franklin. Born the son of a wealthy lawyer and a member of the Vanderbilt family, Hammond could have chosen to lead a pampered life, but when he fell in love with jazz and blues at an early age he decided to devote his life to promoting the music. He was also a civil rights crusader who fought for the rights of coal miners in West Virginia, wrote about the Scottsboro Boys trial for *Nation*, and served on the board of the NAACP.

John Street United Methodist Church—44 John St., lower Manhattan. (212) 269-0014. Established in 1766, this is one of the oldest Methodist churches in the country. A picture of the church's first sexton, Peter Williams, hangs on a wall in the church basement. Williams was a slave whose owner left the country rather than support the Revolution. The church purchased Williams and let him buy his own freedom by working as a sexton.

Kenkeleba House—214-16 E. 2nd St., lower Manhattan. (212) 674-3939. Hours: Wed.-Sat. 11a.m.-6p.m. Founded in 1974, this not-for-profit art organization is dedicated to the preservation of African-American and Third World art that is often overlooked by the mainstream art scene. The name Kenkeleba is derived from the African combretum plant which is believed to have both spiritual and nutritional value. The 6,000 square-foot gallery offers changing exhibits along with art discussions, poetry readings and musical performances. Summer exhibitions focus on African-American artists who are undeservedly obscure.

Lower East Side Tenement Museum—97 Orchard St., lower Manhattan. (212) 431-0233. Hours: Tues.-Fri 11a.m.-4p.m. The country's first museum dedicated to the inner city ethnic experience,

Lower East Side Tenement Museum features several exhibits that interpret the histories of minorities in New York City.

Maiden Lane Slave Uprising Historic Site—Near William Street in lower Manhattan. This is the site of the first organized slave uprising in New York City. Here, on April 12, 1712, about 30 slaves, armed with guns, swords and hatchets, made a desperate bid for freedom. After gathering at an orchard near Maiden Lane, the slaves headed to the house of Peter Van Tilburgh and set it on fire. After a crowd gathered, the slaves opened fire, killing nine of their masters and wounding six others. Soon after, the New York military police converged on the scene, capturing all but six of the slaves. Those who were caught were either hanged or burned alive; the others committed suicide. Following the uprising, harsh laws were drawn up by the City of New York to prevent more uprisings, and blacks were forbidden from owning or inheriting land.

Mary Washington's Residence—79 John St., lower Manhattan. This was the site of the home of Mary Washington, a slave who worked in the New York City home of George Washington. After being freed by George Washington, Mary Washington operated a fruit stand out of her home for almost 30 years. While Washington was still alive, she began annual celebrations in honor of his birthday, and each year displayed in her home personal mementos given to her by him, and invited the public in for a party.

Metropolitan Museum of Art—5th Avenue and 82nd St., Manhattan. (212) 879-5500. Hours: Sun., Tues.-Thur. 9:30a.m.-5:15p.m.; Fri.-Sat. 9:30a.m.-8:45 p.m. Housed behind a monumental facade of Roman arches and Corinthian columns, the Metropolitan is one of the world's greatest museums. The Egyptian exhibit is internationally renowned for its sarcophaguses, hieroglyphics and pottery; and the Michael C. Rockefeller Collection of Art of Africa, Oceana and the Americas is the grandest display of its kind in the world. The Crosby Brown Collection of Musical Instruments of all Nations includes one of the largest assemblages of African musical instruments, including rare and antique lutes made from skulls, ivory horns, thumb pianos, gourd rattles, and animal skin drums. Taped recordings enable viewers to hear the sounds of the instruments as well as view them.

The Metropolitan also has a permanent collection of works by 19th century and contemporary African-American artists such as "Victorian Interior" by Horace Pippin, "The Woodshed" by Romare Bearden, "Blind Beggar" by Jacob Lawrence, sculptures by Richard Barthe, and photographs by Gordon Parks.

Miles Davis' Residence—312 W. 77th St., Manhattan. The legendary trumpeter noted for his cool jazz sounds moved into this red townhouse, a former Russian Orthodox church, in the early 1960s. Davis had the church completely remodeled and installed a music room where he could rehearse without annoying the neighbors. In the early years he lived here with his wife, Frances Taylor, and their children.

While living here Davis recorded several albums including "Miles Smiles," "In a Silent Way," and "Bitches Brew." In 1971 he was named Jazzman of the Year by *Down Beat* magazine. But by the mid-1970s, Davis' life here was less than productive, owing to his drug addiction, poor health, and unhappiness with the music industry. From 1975 to 1980 he dropped out of public view completely, neither recording nor performing. During this time he met actress Cicely Tyson, who is credited with helping him through this difficult period. They were married in 1981, and that same year Davis reemerged as a musician and bandleader. He sold this house soon after. Miles Davis died in 1992 and is buried in Woodlawn Cemetery in the Bronx.

Museum for African Art—593 Broadway, Manhattan. (212) 966-1313. Hours: Wed., Thur., and Sun. 11a.m.-6p.m.; Fri.-Sat. 11a.m.-8p.m. Formerly located on the upper east side, the Museum for African Art presents several intellectually ambitious shows a year. Behind the museum's cast-iron facade, the two-level gallery contains 17,000 square-feet of show space. Designed by Maya Lin, the architect who designed the Vietnam Veteran's Memorial in Washington, D.C., it houses a small permanent collection of pottery, masks, paintings, textiles, drums, and sculpture. Some of the museum's past shows have included "African Masterpieces from Munich," "Africa and the Renaissance," and "Secrecy: African Art That Conceals and Reveals." The museum also has a terrific selection of African art books, catalogs and prints.

Museum of Modern Art—(MOMA) 11 W. 53rd St., Manhattan. (212) 708-9500. Hours: Fri.-Tues. 11a.m.-6p.m., Thur. 11a.m.-9p.m. Founded in 1929, MOMA has an impressive permanent collection of over 100,000 pieces of art. Included are drawings, prints, paintings, photographs, and sculptures by prominent African-American artists, with one of the most impressive being 30 of the 60 panels of "The Migration of the Negro" by social-protest painter Jacob Lawrence.

Nautilus Company Historic Site—58 Wall St., lower Manhattan. This was the original site of the Nautilus Company, one of first insurance companies formed in the U.S. In 1846, a black slave named Philip Swan represented the company's first loss on a policy. Swan was owned by Fred Clarke who had taken out the policy and received the payment following Swan's death. The Nautilus Company is now the New York Life Insurance Company.

Negros Land Historic Site—A 100-square block area stretching from Wall Street to 34th Street, lower Manhattan. During the mid-1600s, this area of lower Manhattan was designated as the "Negros' Land." When the Dutch settlers ran into troubles with the Indians there, they gave the land over to some of their slaves, believing that if the Indians became violent, it would be the blacks who got killed and not them. The Dutch also gave the slaves their freedom on the condition that they supply the Dutch with a yearly allotment of produce. Some of the freed slaves who became prosperous from the new arrangement included Big Manuel, who owned a plot of land that is now near Washington Square Park; and Simon Congo, who owned a 45-acre farm at 14th Street.

New Museum of Contemporary Art—583 Broadway, Manhattan. (212) 219-1222. Hours: Sun., Wed., Thur. noon-6p.m.; Fri.-Sat. noon-8p.m. A collection of powerful images focusing on timely political and social issues including those pertaining to African-Americans. Discussions and dialogues of current exhibits are held on weekends.

Omni Park Central Hotel—870 7th Ave., near W. 55th St., Manhattan. (212) 484-3300. Formerly called the Park Central, this hotel has an impressive history of great jazz performances. In 1928, the Ben Pollack Band, which then included Benny Goodman, performed at the Park Central and the band caused such a sensation that audiences clamored to see them. One night there was an argument between Pollack and band member Jimmy McPartland, and Goodman, disturbed by the fight, quit in a huff. Following the incident, Goodman went on to establish his own band.

Oyster House Historic Site—690 Broadway in Greenwich Village, Manhattan. During the mid-1800s, this location housed a popular seafood restaurant called the Oyster House. The restaurant's African-American owner, George Downing, served as the vice president of the Negro Union and chairman of the 1859 National Convention of Colored Men. Downing was given a gold watch from Queen Victoria after sending her a barrel of his world-famous oysters.

Pierre Toussaint's Grave—Old St. Patrick's Cathedral, 263 Mulberry St., lower Manhattan. (212) 226-8075. In the old graveyard behind this historic church built in 1815 is the grave of Pierre Toussaint, the Haitian-born, anti-slavery and human rights champion.

Race Riots of 1900 Historic Site—The area around 41st Street and 8th Avenue near Times Square, Manhattan. One of the city's early race riots occurred in this area in 1900. The trouble started when a black man shot a white man because he believed the man had molested his wife. The wounded man was a popular policeman in plainclothes, and the incident sparked a racial riot that lasted for several days. Angry white men roamed the streets seeking revenge against any black they met. One of those injured during the riots was Paul Lawrence Dunbar, the noted black poet and writer.

Reisenweber's Restaurant Historic Site—W. 58th Street and 8th Avenue, near Columbus Circle, Manhattan. Although no longer standing, Reisenweber's during the early 1900s was one of the New York clubs responsible for ushering in the Jazz Age. It was at Reisenweber's that the Original Dixieland Jazz Band appeared in 1917, creating a sensation throughout the city. After its appearance at Reisenweber's, the New Orleans band cut "Original Dixieland One-Step" and "Livery Stable Blues," two of its first jazz recordings.

St. George's Episcopal Church— 209 E 16th St., lower Manhattan. (212) 475-0830. This formidable Romanesque Revival brownstone church, sometimes called J.P. Morgan's church, was built in 1856. In addition to J.P. Morgan, other wealthy parishioners included Seth Low and Henry Bacon. What drew many to the church, however, was the baritone soloist Harry T. Burleigh. The son of slaves, Burleigh is often credited with popularizing the black spiritual and adapting the music to the concert stage. He also composed over 300 songs, the most well-known being "Deep River." Later in his life, Burleigh worked with the Czech composer Antonin Dvorak and helped him adapt traditional black melodies into his New World Symphony.

St. Peter's Catholic Church—16 Barclay St., Manhattan. (212) 233-8355. Inside this church, pew number 25 was once reserved for Pierre Toussaint. Toussaint was the freed slave who led the uprising against the French in Haiti, and then went on to become a champion for the poor and homeless in New York City. People from all over the city wrote to Toussaint asking for help, and many of these letters can be found in the main branch of the New York Public Library.

A portrait of Toussaint hangs in the church's rectory. Services are held on Sunday.

St. Peter's Lutheran Church—54th Street and Lexington Avenue, Manhattan. (212) 935-2200. Although it is a Lutheran Church, St. Peter's is also a jazz institution of sorts. For over 25 years, the Reverend John Garcia Gensel has served as pastor, and has attracted an enormous following of jazz lovers and performers. Many jazz musicians have turned to the Reverend in times of trouble. Duke Ellington wrote a poem in his honor, "The Shepard Who Watches Over the Flock," and Billy Strayhorn donated a piano to the church. Gensel has presided over the funerals of many jazz legends including John Coltrane, Thelonious Monk, Eubie Blake, and Alberta Hunter. Big joyous celebrations, the Reverend's funerals have become a popular New York happening that few jazz aficionados miss.

Under the Reverend's direction, the church also sponsors many jazz events including regular jazz concerts on Sunday and Wednesday afternoons, and an annual All-Nite Soul concert held each October. The towering ceilings and stained glass windows offer a wonderfully spiritual setting for soothing jazz sounds.

San Juan Hill Historic Site—W. 60s near 9th Avenue, Manhattan. During the early 1900s, this neighborhood became known as San Juan Hill because of the black veterans of the Spanish-American War who lived here, and also because of the racial conflicts between the blacks and the Irish immigrants in the neighborhood. Many of the black men who lived here at the time worked as stevedores on the Hudson River docks. Eventually, most of the San Juan Hill black population moved up to Harlem.

Scott Joplin's Boarding House Historic Site—252 W. 47th St., Manhattan. From 1911 to 1915, Scott Joplin, the great ragtime composer, operated a boardinghouse here in this small apartment building with his wife, Lottie. At the time it was just a block away from the Hotel Edison, where many of Duke Ellington's musicians stayed. In the front parlor of the boardinghouse, Joplin often played the piano, entertaining the borders as well as himself.

Although today his name is famous, Joplin had some difficult times while living in New York. He suffered from bouts of depression, argued with his publisher, and had problems getting many of his works produced. His classic tune "Maple Leaf Rag" was published in 1899, but the public had not yet embraced ragtime music and it did not become popular until many years later. Joplin, discouraged that his music was not appreciated the way he thought it should be, said at the time "Maybe fifty years after I am dead it will be." In 1970, new recordings of his ragtime compositions were issued. A few years later, a collection of his piano works were published, and his play "Treemonisha" was produced on Broadway.

Slave Market Historic Site—Wall Street near the East River, Manhattan. During the late 1600s, when the British arrived in New York, they erected a slave market here to accommodate the increasing number of slaves being imported by the Royal African Company. At the time, it was one of the busiest slave markets outside of Charleston, South Carolina. By the early 1700s, about 20 percent of the New York City population was comprised of black slaves. Here at this site, the slaves were examined for strength and good health, and sold to the highest bidder.

Stanhope Hotel—995 5th Ave., Manhattan. (212) 288-5800. It was at this midtown hotel, on March 12, 1955, that jazz great Charlie Parker died. He was in the hotel apartment of the Baronness de Koenigswarter, a friend and patron of many jazz musicians, while watching the "Tommy Dorsey Show." Parker was only 34 when he died, but his lifelong abuse of drugs and alcohol caused the medics who found him to estimate his age at 53.

Swing Street Historic Site—52nd Street between 5th and 6th Avenues, Manhattan. From the 1930s to the 1950s, this tiny block was the unofficial gathering spot of musicians. Following Prohibition, New York's jazz scene began to move from Harlem to downtown, and Swing Street, as it was called, was dotted with dozens of popular speakeasies that cradled the talents of such jazz greats as Billie Holiday, Lionel Hampton, and Charlie Parker. The jazz that poured out into the streets included various styles—New Orleans, Chicago, bebop, and cool. Among the other performers who congregated on Swing Street were: Art Tatem, Roy Eldridge, Fats Waller, Dizzie Gillespie, Erroll Garner, Sarah Vaughan, Count Bassie, and Miles Davis. Some of the clubs included: the Onyx, Famous Door, Hickory House, Three Deuces, and Downbeat.

Following World War II, the street started to decline and many of the clubs were turned into burlesque houses. Almost all of the old buildings that once housed the clubs have been replaced with modern skyscrapers, and all that remains of the era are street signs that read "Swing Street" (at 52nd Street between 5th and 6th Avenues) and W.C. Handy Place (at 52nd Street between 6th and 7th Avenues).

Thelonious Monk's Residence—243 W. 63rd St., Manhattan. This red-brick apartment complex behind Lincoln Center is where the noted jazz pianist lived for most of his life. Quiet and introverted, Thelonious Monk was one of modern jazz's true pioneers. Although he was unpredictable and club owners found him difficult to employ, Monk dedicated his life to composing and performing music. He lived here with his wife, Nellie, and their family. Monk stopped performing in 1976, six years before he died. In 1978 he was honored at President Carter's White House Jazz Party. Thelonious Monk is buried in Ferncliff Cemetery in Hartsdale, New York.

Union Square Historic Site—14th to 16th Streets and from 4th Avenue to Broadway in lower Manhattan. During the early 1800s, Union Square was a charming residential square sitting in the center of New York's theater district. It was here, on March 5, 1864, that the Union League Club of New York presented honors to the Twentieth Regiment United States Colored Troops, the first black regiment granted permission to fight in the war. The troops marched down Broadway to the cheers of spectators, until a white officer in the Seventh Regiment said he "refused to let his regiment's band march in front of niggers."

As early as 1861, the African-American citizens of New York asked for the opportunity to enlist in the New York regiments of the Union Army. At the time, the Confederacy allowed the enlisting of blacks, but neither President Lincoln nor the Northern states called upon blacks for their help. As a result, during the mid-1800s, New York blacks traveled to other states in order to enlist. By the end of the Civil War, over 800 black New Yorkers died in battle with the Union troops.

Waldorf Astoria—Park Avenue at E. 49th Street, Manhattan. One of New York's grandest hotels, the Waldorf has had its share of important jazz events. During the late 1930s and 1940s, Charlie Parker played here, and it was at the Waldorf in 1971 that Louis Armstrong gave his last concert performance.

Warren Street Historic Site—51 Warren St., lower Manhattan. This is the former site of the home of Katy Ferguson. The daughter of a slave, Ferguson adopted 20 white children and 28 black children. She was instrumental in New York City's Sunday School movement and helped establish better conditions for orphaned children in New York City.

W.C. Handy Music Publishing Co. Historic Site— 1650 Broadway, Manhattan. W.C. Handy, often called the father of the blues, owned and operated his music publishing company at this site in the early 1900s.

Whitney Museum of American Art—945 Madison Ave., Manhattan. (212) 570-3676. Hours: Wed.-Sat. 11a.m.-5p.m., Tues. 1-8p.m., Sun. noon-5p.m. For over 50 years, the Whitney has held an impressive collection of American art and information on living artists. Inside, mysterious stairways lead into spacious, indirectly lit galleries. Included in the museum's 6,500 piece collection are works by African-American artists Jacob Lawrence and Charles White, and the graceful statue entitled "The Blackberry Woman" by Richmond Barthe.

SHOPPING, DINING & ENTERTAINMENT

Abyssinia Restaurant—35 Grand St., Manhattan. (212) 226-5959. Lunch on weekends and dinner nightly. An informal and pleasant eatery specializing in authentic and very spicy Ethiopian foods. Dishes include flat injera bread, chicken stew, collard greens with ginger, steak tartare, spiced vegetables, and chocolate truffles.

Alvin Ailey American Dance Theater—1515 Broadway, Manhattan. (212) 997-1975. The world renown modern dance company performs several times a year at various theaters. Founded in 1958, the company premiered what has been called Ailey's masterwork "Revelations" in 1960, and has gone on to enthrall audiences around the world ever since.

Alvin Ailey, born into a poor Texas family in 1931, started studying dance in Los Angeles while still in high school. In 1949 he studied with noted modern dance instructor Lester Horton, and eventually went on to study in New York with Martha Graham. During the 1950s he performed in Harry Belafonte's "Sing, Man, Sing" and was the lead dancer in "Jamaica," starring Lena Horne and Ricardo Montalban. Following his stage successes, Ailey formed his own company.

Although Ailey was criticized by many African-Americans for having an integrated dance company, he insisted that his multicultural company would break down many racial barriers and stereotypes about dancing and race. He proved that white dancers can dance the blues, Japanese dancers can execute jazz technique, and black dancers can perform classical ballet. In 1984, the company became the first mostly black modern dance company to perform a two-week season at the Metropolitan Opera House. Alvin Ailey died in 1989 in New York. Following his death one of the company's most famous members, Judith Jamison, was chosen to take over as the new director.

Arthur's Tavern—57 Grove St., Greenwich Village, Manhattan. (212) 675-6879. A classic jazz joint with a well-worn wooden bar and twinkling Christmas lights, Arthur's is housed in a building that dates to the early 1800s. Featuring jazz since the 1940s, the cozy and dark club has two house bands that attract jazz lovers nightly.

Ashione Art Gallery—269 W. 4th St., lower Manhattan. (212) 229-0899. Hours: Tues.-Thur. noon-7p.m., Fri.-Sun. noon-8p.m. This is a fine gallery featuring museum quality African works of art including sculptures, oils, masks, artifacts, batiks, Kente cloth, jewelry and bronze works.

Birdland—2745 Broadway, upper Manhattan. (212) 749-2228. Although not as good as the original Birdland club made famous during the 1950s, this upscale jazz club features top rate performers and a spicy Cajun-style menu, and attracts a loyal, local crowd. Live music nightly and during brunch on Sundays.

Black Books Plus—702 Amsterdam Ave., at 94th St., Manhattan. (212) 749-9632. Hours: Tues.-Fri. 11a.m.-6p.m., Sat. 11a.m.-5:30p.m. A good assortment of new, used and out of print books relating to African-American history and culture.

Blue Nile Restaurant—103 W. 77th St., Manhattan. (212) 580-3232. Lunch and dinner. Not just an Ethiopian restaurant, Blue Nile is an Ethiopian experience that sends the uninformed into culture shock. The decor includes authentic Ethiopian art and carvings, and seating is on tiny, squat stools barely a foot from the ground. The inexpensive menu is exotic: fresh injera bread, spicy lentil stew, ginger spiced chick-pea puree, lamb stew, garlic-ginger chicken, raw chopped beef seasoned with chili powder, and sweet honey wine.

Blue Note—131 W. 3rd St., Greenwich Village, Manhattan. (212) 475-8592. Music nightly. One of New York's most popular jazz supper clubs, the Blue Note, although expensive, crowded, and a bit too commercial, is a first-rate spot for mainstream jazz acts. In past years, many big names performed here including Sarah Vaughan, Dizzy Gillespie, and Joe Williams. Monday nights are reserved for amateur acts, and brunches are served on weekends with a special "Soul Brunch" on Saturdays. The best jazz at the Blue Note, according to regulars, often takes place after hours following the last scheduled set. Reservations are suggested.

Bottom Line—15 W. 4th St., Greenwich Village, Manhattan. (212) 228-6300. A huge Village hang-out with dozens of tables and live jazz, blues and popular music nightly. The club's varied list of entertainment has included: Muddy Waters, B.B. King, Miles Davis, Stevie Wonder, Lou Reed, George Benson, Grover Washington, Jr., and Prince. Reservations suggested on weekends.

Bradley's—70 University Pl., lower Manhattan. (212) 473-9700. According to *Newsday* jazz critic Stuart Troup, Bradley's is the finest piano-bass room in the world. The piano is tuned daily to keep it in perfect condition, and the club's acoustics allow for a pleasant conversation as well as some fine-sounding jazz. Most nights the club features duos and trios with Sunday night dedicated to avant-garde experimentation. Bradley's serves food till 2a.m., and musicians who are just getting off from work elsewhere often come in for a bite. Reservations suggested on weekends.

B. Smith's—771 8th Ave., at 47th Street, Manhattan. (212) 247-2222. Lunch and dinner. A stylish eatery with live jazz on weekends and American cuisine. Definitely a hit with New York's young, black professional crowd.

Cafe Carlyle—Hotel Carlyle, Madison Avenue and 76th Street, Manhattan. (212) 744-1600. An elegant and intimate jazz room that has featured jazzman Bobby Short for 25 years, the Carlyle also offers other fine jazz pianists and classic cabaret acts nightly except Sunday. Reservations suggested.

Caribe—117 Perry St., Manahttan. (212) 255-9191. Dinner. With authentic Caribbean dishes, Caribe is a West Indian happening set amid lush indoor plants. Generous, inexpensive platters of specialties from various islands include: stewed fish, curried chicken, boiled bananas, Cuban pork, and conch fritters. Drinks include fresh sour sop juice, ginger beer, and potent rum punch.

Carlos I—432 6th Ave., lower Manhattan. (212) 982-3260. A comfortable and pleasant supper club that features mainstream jazz that never gets too loud, and spicy Caribbean food. Reservations suggested.

Chez Josephine—414 W. 42nd St., Manhattan. (212) 594-1925. Dinner, closed Sunday. A tribute to the dazzling dancer who took Paris by storm in 1925, Chez Josephine is a sophisticated French bistro adorned with posters, paintings, caricatures and sepia photos of the scantily clad Josephine Baker. The restaurant opened on October 2, 1986, the date of Baker's opening at the famous Theatre de Champs Elysee in Paris, in 1925. French host Jean-Claude Baker, Josephine Baker's adopted son, sees to it that the restaurant maintains a 1920s Paris atmosphere, the baby grand is played nightly, the wine list is top notch, and the patrons are always pampered. Choice items on the menu include: poached leeks, lobster cassoulet, french-fried sweet potatoes, blood pudding, and spaghetti Josephine. Reservations suggested.

Dan Lynch—221 2nd Ave., lower Manhattan. (212) 677-0911. One of the oldest blues bars in New York, Dan Lynch is a casual and cozy gathering spot with dim lights and rickety tables. The bar dates back to Prohibition days, when it was owned by two Irish brothers. Today, it features local blues bands that often have a touch of gospel. Live music nightly with jam sessions on Sundays.

Delta 88—332 8th Ave., Manhattan. (212) 924-3499. A soul food restaurant and R&B club, Delta 88 has a funky Southern atmosphere that attracts a varied clientele including celebrities such as Mick Jagger and Bruce Springsteen. Dancing is common, and along with local R&B bands, the club also offers zydeco and gospel. Live music nightly.

Fat Tuesday's—190 3rd Ave., Manhattan. (212) 533-7902. Lunch and dinner. Housed in a building constructed in 1894, Fat Tuesday's offers an all-American menu of burgers and sandwiches amid a decor of Tiffany-style lamps and old, vaudeville photos. Major jazz acts nightly including occasional appearances by Betty "Bebop" Carter, and jazz brunches on Sunday.

Fifty-five Bar—55 Christopher St., Greenwich Village, Manhattan. (212) 929-9883. An old, dingy bar that dates back to Prohibition, the 55 Bar is a tiny, below-the-ground gathering spot that occasionally offers live jazz. Its jukebox, however, has one of the best collections of jazz classics in New York.

Fortune Garden Pavilion—209 E. 49th St., Manhattan. (212) 753-0101. Dinner. An odd combination part Chinese restaurant and part jazz club the Fortune Garden offers live piano jazz trios Tuesday through Sunday, with first-rate Chinese food. Reservations suggested.

Green Street Cafe—103 Green St., midtown Manhattan. (212) 925-2415. A former sanitation truck garage reborn as a jazz cafe featuring live piano and bass duos in the restaurant downstairs and jazz vocalists in a lounge upstairs.

Henry Street Settlement New Federal Theater—466 Grand St., lower Manhattan. (212) 598-0400. A fine theater company that has hosted many plays produced on Broadway including Ntozake Shange's "Women Who've Considered Suicide..."

Honeysuckle Restaurant—507 Columbus Ave., Manhattan. (212) 496-8095. Dinners nightly and brunch on Saturday and Sunday with a variety of live music including jazz. Pure Southern specialties amid a romantic country decor of stone fireplaces and indoor lamp posts. The menu includes: Salmon cakes, blueberry pancakes, smothered chicken, turkey and stuffing, black-eyed peas, sweet potato pie, chopped pork barbecue, and banana pudding.

Indigo Blues—221 W. 46th St., Manhattan. (212) 221-0033. A theater district jazz club with a dark yet glitzy atmosphere, Indigo Blues with its high-tech stage offers big name jazz, blues and R&B acts nightly, such as Regina Belle, Bobbi Humphrey, and Alyson Williams. Reservations suggested.

Jezebel's Restaurant—304 E. 50th St., Manhattan. (212) 582-1045. Dinner. A theater district treat with Tiffany lamps, fringed shawls, wicker chairs, piano music and Old South atmosphere. New Orleans-style Southern dishes include: deep fried catfish, she-crab soup, smothered pork chops, creamy potato salad, and whiskey laced bread pudding. Reservations suggested.

June Kelly Gallery—591 Broadway, third floor, lower Manhattan. (212) 226-1660. Hours: Tues.-Sat. 11a.m.-6p.m. Closed in August except by appointment. One of the first commercial art galleries in New York's SoHo area owned by a black woman, the June Kelly Gallery features shows by established and emerging African-American artists including sculpture, paintings, collages, and ceramics. June Kelly, director of the gallery, was once a manager for the noted African-American artist Romare Bearden.

Knickerbocker Restaurant—33 University Pl., Greenwich Village, Manhattan. (212) 228-8490. Dinner. An old, all-American eatery that features 28-ounce Porterhouse steaks and live piano and bass duos that are described by the restaurant's manager as ideal for the "novice jazz listener."

Lola's Restaurant—30 W. 22nd St., Manhattan. (212) 675-6700. Lunch and dinner. A serene setting with brass lamps, a busy bar, and a garden view. Sunday brunch includes live gospel music and is a favorite after church happening. Southern, Cajun and Caribbean specialties include: shrimp and potato fritters, chicken curry, cayenne onion rings, crab cakes, 100 spice fried chicken, plantain chips, cabbage slaw, ham steak, black-eyed peas, and collard greens. Reservations suggested.

Lone Star Roadhouse—240 W. 52nd St., Manhattan. (212) 245-2950. Formerly a Greenwich Village hang-out, the Lone Star moved uptown recently, but still has an American-roots atmosphere. The first New York City club to feature big name country western performers, the Lone Star features blues, zydeco, and rockabilly music nightly. Reservations suggested on weekends.

Manny's Car Wash—1558 3rd Ave., Manhattan. (212) 369-2583. A small, intimate and dark blues club that offers both local and national blues acts Tuesday through Sunday.

Mehu Art Gallery—21 W. 100th St., upper Manhattan. (212) 222-3334. Hours: Tues.-Fri. 11a.m.-3p.m. and 5-7:30 p.m., Sat.-Sun. noon-6p.m. Owned and operated by Haitian-born Herve Mehu, this small and friendly gallery features a good assortment of primitive Haitian art and usually has lively Haitian music playing in the background to set the mood. It also has a fine collection of prominent African-American artists such as Romare Bearden.

Merton D. Simpson Gallery—1064 Madison Ave., Manhattan. (212) 988-6290. Hours: Tues.-Sat. 10:30a.m-5:30p.m. and by appointment. Mertie Simpson is one of New York's most respected African art dealers and his gallery features an outstanding collection of authentic sculptures, masks and decorative art.

Mr. Leo's Restaurant—17 W. 27th St., Manhattan. (212) 532-6673. Lunch and dinner. A romantic, genteel Old South eatery with fresh flowers and excellent service. Authentic Southern dishes include: honey-dipped fried chicken, short ribs in gravy, cream of collard green soup, fried catfish, chitlins and champagne, banana pie, and peach cobbler. Reservations suggested.

Mo' Better Restaurant—570 Amsterdam Ave., Manhattan. (212) 580-7755. Dinner. A soul food eatery with a cool decor of bold colors, a mirrored bar, pool tables, and live jazz Thursday through

Saturday. Items on the menu include catfish fingers, okra and salmon soup, barbecue pork ribs, country steak, and vegetarian platters.

National Opera Ebony—2109 Broadway, Manhattan. (212) 877-2110. In residence at City College's Aaron Davis Hall, this multicultural opera company has toured throughout the United States and Europe, and performs regularly at various locations in New York City. Its 25 singers, accompanied by dancers, offer a variety of productions including contemporary music, spirituals, and classic works such as "Figaro" and "La Traviata."

Negro Ensemble Company—Theater Four, W. 55th St., Manhattan. (212) 246-8545. A preeminent theater company that produces three new works annually focusing on African-American culture and history.

Ngone Sengalese Restaurant—823 6th Ave., near 28th Street, Manhattan. (212) 967-7899. Lunch and diner. An authentic African restaurant decorated with African artifacts, batik fabrics, and tropical plants, Ngone attracts many United Nations officials and visiting Africans. With soft African music playing in the background, its spicy menu features: fishballs, foufou dumplings, yams, akura, black-eyed peas, stuffed patties, sorrel and ginger drinks.

Pink Teacup Restaurant—42 Grove St., Manhattan. (212) 807-6755. Breakfast, lunch and dinner. A cozy and quaint soul food cafe decorated with photographs of famous patrons Sammy Davis, Jr., Sarah Vaughan, and Chaka Khan. For over 25 years, the Pink Teacup has attracted crowds who dine on its Southern specialties such as Cornish hens and wild rice, giblet stew, black-eyed peas and okra, spicy chopped barbecue beef, and sweet potato pie.

Rainbow Room—30 Rockefeller Plaza, Manhattan. (212) 632-5000. Located high above midtown Manhattan, the Rainbow Room is a New York institution with great views of the city, a revolving dance floor, and waiters dressed in pastel suits. Completely renovated in the late 1980s, the late-night continental supper club features big band entertainment including live jazz nightly, except Mondays. Reservations suggested.

Red Blazer Too Restaurant—349 W. 46th St., Manhattan. (212) 262-3112. Dinner nightly and brunch on Sunday. A comfortable, old-fashioned kind of place that features an array of live traditional jazz, big band swing, Dixieland, and ragtime piano nightly. The large theater district club offers an all-American menu of steaks, burgers and chops.

Revolution Bookstore—13 E. 16th St., Manhattan. (212) 691-3345. Hours: Mon.-Sat. 10a.m.-7p.m. This non-profit bookstore staffed with volunteers has a very liberal social conscience. Books are organized by categories including black family; African-American history; black struggles in the United States, Haiti and South America; and the oppression of women. It also has a large assortment of alternative press magazines.

Robertson African Arts—36 W. 22nd St., 4th floor, Manhattan. (212) 675-4045. By appointment only. An elegant and sophisticated gallery specializing in exquisite African art. All pieces are for sale including authentic fertility dolls, 14th century bronze bells, hardwood masks, and carvings.

Roseland Ballroom—239 W. 52nd St., Manhattan. (212) 247-0200. While not as glamorous as the original Roseland Ballroom formerly at 1658 Broadway, the new Roseland represents a slice of New York history that has remained despite the odds. It was at the old Roseland, one of the largest ballrooms in New York from the 1920s through the 1940s, that big name bands mesmerized the crowds and set the scene for the lavish dancing shows that became world famous. During its heyday, gentlemen in fine suits bought a ten-cent ticket that allowed them to dance with a Roseland hostess. Among the legendary acts that performed at Roseland were Count Bassie and Fletcher Henderson's band (which included Louis Armstrong for a while). Roseland, however, was a segregated club that disallowed Hispanics as well as blacks from admission. Although much of the old glory is gone, today's Roseland still features ball-room dancing, an endangered species on the dance scene, along with live, Big Band music. Three times a week, starting in early afternoon, couples gather to dance under the domed ceiling. Near the entrance is a "Dance City Hall of Fame," with displays of dancing shoes once belonging to Bill "Bojangles" Robinson and Gregory Hines; and a plaque listing the now-married couples who met and fell in love at the ballroom.

Shark Bar—307 Amsterdam Ave., Manhattan. (212) 874-8500. Lunch, dinner and an all-you-can-eat Sunday buffet. Wood floors and brick walls set the mood for this cozy eatery. The menu changes often but soul food specialties such as ribs, fried chicken, candied yams, and macaroni and cheese are always available.

S.O.B.'s—204 Varick St., lower Manhattan. (212) 243-4940. A lively dance club that attracts an upscale, multicultural crowd, S.O.B.'s features live African, Caribbean, Brazilian and jazz music Monday through Saturday amid an exotic decor of straw huts, bamboo, and imitation palm trees.

Sweet Basil—88 7th Ave. S., Greenwich Village, Manhattan. (212) 242-1785. A split-level, glass encased room, Basil's is a comfortable and pleasant jazz club that is never too noisy or crowded. Jazz photos grace the walls and candle-light creates an intimate setting. Opened in 1981 by a singer from the Bronx, a jazz promoter from Berlin, and a former school principal, Basil's has had many albums recorded from jam sessions on its stage. The music varies from classic cool to avant-garde, and brunches are offered on Sundays. Reservations are suggested.

Sweetwaters—170 Amsterdam Ave., Manhattan. (212) 873-4100. Lunch and dinner. Although primarily a continental menu, Sweet-waters features live jazz and rhythm and blues acts nightly.

Town Hall—123 W. 43rd St., Manhattan. (212) 840-2824. A concert hall that frequently features jazz concerts, Town Hall is where Charlie Parker gave his last public concert in 1954. One of the oldest, still-operating jazz clubs in the city, Town Hall began offering jazz in the early 1940s.

Tramps—45 W. 21st St., Manhattan. (212) 727-7788. Formerly a seedy hole-in-the-wall blues joint, Tramps has been transformed into a big, beautiful club that even has linen table cloths. It still, however, features some of the finest blues and R&B acts in the city including Otis Rush and Big Joe Turner. Live music Thursday through Sunday with American food. Reservations suggested on weekends.

United Nations Gift Shop—At the 1st Avenue and 46th Street entrance of the United Nations, midtown Manhattan. (212) 963-1234. Hours: daily 9a.m.-5p.m. In addition to an assortment of souvenirs from around the world, the U.N. gift shop also has an array of handmade crafts and dolls from several African countries.

University Place Book Store—821 Broadway, near 12th Street, lower Manhattan. (212) 254-5998. Hours: Mon.-Fri. 10a.m.-5p.m., Sat. 11a.m.-1p.m. A crowded and dusty book shop and resource center with one of the most comprehensive collections of books on the African Diaspora. Also, vintage copies of *Ebony* from the 1950s, and hundreds of rare and out-of-print books.

Village Corner—Bleecker Street and LaGuardia Place, Greenwich Village, Manhattan. (212) 473-9762. An old standard in the New York jazz scene, the Village Corner is housed in a 19th century building at what is often called the "Corner of Walk and Don't Walk."

The story told at the club is that in 1951 a patron of the bar had too much to drink. When he called his wife to come pick him up and she asked where he was, he looked up, saw the sign and said "The corner of walk and don't walk." The club's location is listed in the New York City phone book as at the corner of Walk and Don't Walk. The Village Corner offers mainstream piano jazz nightly with an atmosphere of ceiling fans, dark walls and an old wooden bar.

Village Gate—160 Bleecker St., near Thompson, Greenwich Village, Manhattan. (212) 475-5120. One of the most highly regarded jazz and cabaret clubs in New York, the Village Gate hosts well-known jazz and blues acts as well as occasional salsa bands. Housed in a luxury apartment building, the club is divided into three parts: the Top of the Gate which features cabaret and revues, the Terrace which features small groups, and the 450-seat lower level Gate which features well known jazz and blues acts. Over 60 albums have been recorded at the Village Gate and its list of legendary performers includes: Dizzy Gillespie, Charles Mingus, John Lee Hooker, B.B. King, Miles Davis, and Otis Rush. In recent years, the club has featured several off-Broadway plays including *One Mo' Time* and *Further Mo'*. Reservations are suggested.

Village Vanguard—178 7th Ave. S., Greenwich Village, Manhattan. (212) 255-4037. Live music nightly. One of the oldest jazz clubs in New York, the Village Vanguard is a quintessential music experience. Dark, smoky, and crowded, with faded pictures of jazz legends, the tiny club continues to offer great music and attract jazz lovers from around the world.

In the good-old-days, John Coltrane, Dinah Washington, Sonny Rollins, Eartha Kitt, Thelonious Monk, Charles Mingus, and Miles Davis all played here. Opened in 1934, the Vanguard started out as a casual hang-out for artists and writers, but by the 1950s it was a jazz institution. Today, the club still offers the finest talent available, usually performing classic jazz of the 1940s and '50s. Reservations suggested.

West End Gate—2911 Broadway, upper Manhattan. (212) 662-8830. Affiliated with the Village Gate jazz club, the West End Gate features top-rate jazz acts in a dark and comfortable room. Music nightly.

Wonderland Blues Bar & Restaurant—519 2nd Ave., lower Manhattan. (212) 213-5098. Dinner. A neighborhood blues joint that has recently gone a bit upscale, Wonderland features live blues, jazz, and R&B groups nightly except Monday, and offers a Southern-style menu. Reservations suggested on weekends.

Manhattan

Zanzibar & Grill—550 3rd Ave., Manhattan. (212) 779-0606. Dinner. An American-food restaurant with an elegant, tropical African atmosphere that attracts an upscale, fashionable crowd. Live music nightly includes jazz, blues, zydeco, and Cajun. Reservations suggested.

Chapter 2

Harlem

*J*ust the mention of Harlem beings to mind a melange of diverse images: steamy jazz clubs, soap-box preachers, exotic dancers, Renaissance poets, gospel choirs, street-wise pimps, brownstone mansions, and urban blight. At the northern tip of the island of Manhattan, Harlem is full of contradictions. Yes, it has its share of inner-city problems, but Harlem is also a place where mothers walk with baby carriages, little girls play double-dutch, and grandmothers sweep their front porches clean every morning. It is a place where the aroma of hamhocks simmering in collard greens wafts through the air, and the pulsating rhythms of rap music reverberate from the pavement. Harlem is America's most-recognized neighborhood, and it is often misunderstood. Bounded by 170th Street to the north, 96th Street to the south, the Harlem and East Rivers to the east, and the Hudson River to the west, Harlem is considered by many to be the cradle of African-American culture. The list of prominent blacks who were either born in Harlem, or at one time lived there, is staggering: Alvin Ailey, James Baldwin, Harry Belafonte, Eubie Blake, Cab Calloway, Diahann Carrol, Ernest Chrichlow, John Henrik Clarke, Sammy Davis, Jr., Ruby Dee, David N. Dinkins, W.E.B. DuBois, Duke Ellington, Ella Fitzgerald, Marcus Garvey, Althea Gibson, Lionel Hampton, Jimi Hendrix, Langston Hughes, Zora Neale Hurston, Scott Joplin, Jacob Lawrence, Joe Louis,

Harlem

Thurgood Marshall, Willie Mays, Charlie Parker, Gordon Parks, Adam Clayton Powell, Jr., Sidney Poitier, Bill "Bojangles" Robinson, James VanDerZee, Fats Waller, Ethel Waters, Billy Dee Williams, Richard Wright, and Malcom X. Established by the Dutch in 1658 and originally called Nieuw Haarlem, the name was Anglicized in 1664 when the land fell to the British. Harlem, however, remained a Dutch farming community for about 200 years. But in the early 1800s things began to change. In 1837 the Harlem Railroad arrived, and in 1873 Harlem was annexed to the city. By the early 1900s Harlem became an affluent New York City suburb where upper-class whites lived in plush brick townhouses surrounded by manicured gardens and towering trees. And then once again things changed. The extension of the rapid transit system, now reaching all the way to Lenox Avenue, brought an influx of European immigrants and African-Americans to the neighborhood. By 1910, blacks were forced out of their mid-Manhattan neighborhoods and many began the slow but steady move up to Harlem that would continue for years to come. Fearful of the racial changes taking place in the neighborhood, most of the upper-class whites fled.

During the 1920s and '30s, Harlem established itself as a predominantly black middle-class neighborhood and bustling center for African-American creativity. The era known as the Harlem Renaissance was in full bloom, and nowhere else in America could so many gifted, young blacks be found. In an area of just a few square miles, artists, writers, poets, musicians, singers, actors, and dancers all lived and worked together creating one of the most incredible cultural and literary explosions ever to hit the United States. It was also during this time that Harlem developed an international reputation as a glamorous playground that attracted hordes of curious whites who came to marvel at the exotic clubs and cabarets. The Cotton Club and Savoy Ballroom were the rage, reveling in the so-called Jazz Age and New Negro movement that set a standard for entertainment throughout the world.

BLACK NEW YORK

The music and the liquor kept on flowing even during the war years of the 1940s, but during the 1950s urban decay began taking its toll. Many of the famous clubs closed down and a large portion of the middle-class residents abandoned the neighborhood. During the turbulent civil rights era of the 1960s, Harlem was an influential mecca of intellectual and social consciousness. The tense streets were the scene for numerous public protests and political demonstrations causing even more of the middle-class residents to move to less volatile New York City neighborhoods. During the 1980s, historic preservationists came to the rescue and good things began to happen. Many of the old brownstones were turned into upscale condominiums complete with flower boxes full of geraniums and refurbished iron grill-work. These days, Harlem is once again a vibrant neighborhood and a very livable place. Its diverse population includes writers, artists, musicians, bankers, lawyers, yuppies, buppies, and old-timers who never left. Divided into three distinct sections, Harlem today includes: West Harlem, also called Spanish Harlem, where many Hispanics live; East Harlem, which has more white residents than the other two; and Central Harlem, where the population is predominantly African-American and most of the historic sites and cultural centers can be found.

Music remains the heartbeat of Harlem, and the ever-present sounds of jazz, blues and gospel are still an important part of the neighborhood's character. The world-famous Cotton Club and Apollo Theater have both been brought back to life, proving that good things rarely die. Shiny stretch limousines carry dedicated downtown customers to Sylvia's soul food restaurant where the smothered pork chops and candied yams attract a full house every night. Bus loads of European and Japanese tourists pass through on tours, as neighborhood kids play stick ball in the streets. Harlem today is chock-full of sights, sounds and smells that almost always leave first-time visitors determined to come back for more.

HISTORIC SITES AND CULTURAL CENTERS

Abysinnian Baptist Church—132 W. 138th St. between Lenox Avenue and Adam Clayton Powell, Jr., Boulevard, Harlem. (212) 862-7474. A member of the independent black Baptist churches founded by Thomas Paul in 1808, the Abysinnian Baptist Church was established here in 1921 and opened its doors in 1924. The magnificent Gothic and Tudor structure with its stained-glass windows, circular pews, red carpet, and marble pulpit is constructed out of New York bluestone and has one of the largest black congregations in the country.

One of the church's most well known leaders was Adam Clayton Powell, Jr., who arrived in New York City when he was 12-years-old at the time his father assumed the pastorate of the church. The senior Powell had risen from poverty in Virginia to a degree at Yale, but the church he took over was small and debt-ridden. Within a few years, he turned it into one of the largest Protestant congregations in the country.

Powell, Jr., a pioneer in the civil rights movement and the first black member of Congress from an eastern state, took over as pastor in 1930 following his father's retirement. In addition to serving as pastor, Powell, Jr., took over the church's free meal program and within a few months had set up social service programs throughout Harlem. This work evolved into a series of community protests, demanding that white businessmen hire black workers. A charismatic character, Powell, Jr., was credited with empowering much of the Harlem community during the Great Depression and securing jobs for blacks in some of New York's biggest companies. He also advocated desegregation of the armed forces and attacked Jim Crow practices in Washington, D.C. Although his flamboyant style delighted some, it also infuriated many others. He was stripped of his committee chairmanship in the House of Representatives on charges of misconduct and was rejected at the polls. After his death, however, one of the main streets in Harlem was renamed in his honor. The church houses a small museum in honor of Powell's contribution.

Another noted minister of the church was Fats Waller's father, and it was at the Abysinnian Baptist Church that Charlie Parker's funeral was held. Reverend Dr. Calvin Butts, a Harlem community activist, now serves as pastor. Lively Sunday morning services are held complete with contemporary gospel and choir music. The church's five-keyboard organ is said to be the largest in New York City.

African American Wax Museum—316 W. 115th St., Harlem. (212) 678-7818. Hours: Tues.-Sun. 1-6p.m. An offbeat, privately run museum housed in an old brownstone, this museum is surrounded by painted bathtubs full of plants. Inside, artist Raven Chanticleer displays his life-like wax figures of heroes such as Malcolm X, Dr. Martin Luther King, Jr., and Nelson Mandela.

Afro Arts Cultural Center—2191 Adam Clayton Powell, Jr., Blvd., Harlem. (212) 996-3333. Hours: daily 9a.m.-5p.m. A cultural and educational center with an art gallery and African museum that offers jazz concerts, African dance performances, and African culture workshops. Founded by Simon Bly, Jr., in 1947, the center is also active in the United Nations Children's World Conference.

Alhambra Theater Historic Site—2110 Adam Clayton Powell, Jr., Blvd., near 126th Street, Harlem. A popular jazz and blues club during the 1930s, the Alhambra Theater was where a young John Hammond, who later went on to become a record producer and music critic, saw his first live blues performer the legendary Bessie Smith. Billie Holiday, during her early performing years, also played at the Alhambra. Across the street from the theater was the Alhambra Grill, another music venue. The Alhambra Theater is now an office building.

American Academy and Institute of Arts and Letters—633 W. 155th St., just north of Harlem. (212) 368-5900. The institute sponsors three excellent exhibits a year, focusing on paintings, sculptures and manuscripts, including the works of prominent African-Americans.

A. Philip Randolph Square—Where 7th Avenue and St. Nicholas Avenue intersect at 117th Street. A. Philip Randolph was instrumental in organizing the Brotherhood of Sleeping Car Porters which brought a sense of dignity to the many African-American railroad porters who worked on the country's trains. In 1941 he persuaded President Franklin D. Roosevelt to establish the Fair Employment Practices Commission which made it possible for blacks to work in defense jobs which had previously been barred to them.

In former years, Randolph Square was called Dewey Square because it was once the location of the old Dewey Square Hotel. Dewey Square was where the great jazz artist Charlie Parker got the inspiration for his song of the same name.

Apollo Theater—See listing in Shopping, Dining & Entertainment section.

Astor Row—8-62 W. 130th St., between 5th and Lenox Avenues, Harlem. This collection of historic, three-story single-family row houses was built in the late 1880s by John J. Astor, one of the wealthiest landlords in New York City. Currently undergoing a major restoration, the two dozen houses, complete with covered wooden porches, were designated as historic landmarks by New York City in 1981.

The "A" Train—145th Street near St. Nicholas Avenue (among other stops), Harlem. The world-famous "A" train was the fastest and easiest way to get to Harlem when the jazz scene was jumping in the neighborhood. The "A" train line had just been completed when composer Billy Strayhorn wrote the song that would make Duke Ellington famous.

Audubon Ballroom Historic Site—166th Street and Broadway, Harlem. No longer in existence, the Audubon Ballroom was the site where the 39-year-old black nationalist leader Malcolm X was shot and killed on February 21, 1965. Although community organizations tried to save the structure from demolition in 1993, they were defeated. Columbia University is planning to build a research center on the site and preserve a portion of the building as a Malcolm X memorial.

Aunt Len's Doll and Toy Museum—6 Hamilton Terr., at 141st Street, Harlem. (212) 926-4172. By appointment only. Here, down in the basement of an old Harlem brownstone, is an ecclectic collection of dolls owned by retired school teacher Lenon Holder Hoyte—more commonly known as Aunt Len. Hoyte began collecting dolls in 1962 and her collection is now one of the largest in the world. It includes dolls made of wood, leather, fabric, china, wax, and papier-mache. Along with the Betty Boops and Howdy Doodys are numerous multi-cultural dolls from around the world, Aunt Jemimas, black baby dolls, and even one of Muhammad Ali.

Baby Grand Historic Site—319 W. 125th St., near Frederick Douglass Boulevard, Harlem. For over 40 years, the Baby Grand was a lively and popular cabaret that hosted musicians such as Joe Turner and Jimmy Butts, as well as comedian Nipsey Russell. In 1988, blues singer Ruth Brown taped a birthday show at the Baby Grand for national television. The Baby Grand closed in 1989 and is now a store.

Billie Holiday's First New York Residence—108 W. 139th St., near Lenox Avenue, Harlem. This bleak five-story apartment building is where Billie Holiday lived with her mother, Sadie, when she first came to New York. Holiday's mother was unmarried and having difficulty supporting herself, let alone her daughter. It was during the Great Depression and times were hard. To bring money into the household, Sadie started cooking for a living and turned their apartment into an informal soup kitchen and hang-out for down-and-out musicians who came by for home-made fried chicken and a shot of whiskey.

While living here, Holiday searched for work until she finally found a job at a small club called Pod's and Jerry's on West 132nd

Street. Although she auditioned as a dancer, her dancing skills were far from adequate, and the club hired her instead as a singer. Only a teenager, Holiday began singing regular gigs throughout Harlem and borrowed from the jazz and blues styles she heard other singers performing. By 1933, she was singing in the then popular Harlem club called Monette's.

Finally, in 1935 Holiday got the chance to perform at the Apollo Theater and her blues singing, ripe with pain and loneliness, brought down the house. Soon after she was producing records, performing at other clubs, and rising to the top of the blues charts. After years of battling with drug addiction and alcoholism, Holiday died in New York in 1959 at the age of 44.

Black Fashion Museum—155 W. 126th St., Harlem. (212) 666-1320. By appointment only. Behind the reinforced metal door of this partially renovated two-story brownstone sits a stunning collection of garments designed, sewn or worn by African-Americans. The collection includes over 3,000 dresses, shoes, hats and photos dating from the mid-1800s to the present. Founded by Louis K. Alexander, the museum includes mannequins dressed in an assortment of costumes from ballgowns to christening suits and day dresses. On the second floor are a reproduction of the purple velvet inaugural gown worn by Mary Todd Lincoln and designed by a former slave, and the yellow floral print dress Rosa Parks had been sewing that day in 1955 when she refused to give up her seat on a Montgomery, Alabama, bus. Also in the museum are the costumes from the shows "The Wiz," "Eubie," and "Bubbling Brown Sugar;" and a collection of African garments and fabrics.

Along with the fashions themselves, the museum highlights the vast number of African-Americans who have contributed to fashion, such as Ann Lowe, the designer of the wedding gown Jacqueline Bouvier wore when she married John F. Kennedy. The Black Fashion Museum is located next door to the Harlem Institute of Fashion, a non-profit fashion school also founded by Louis K. Alexander.

Black Swan Record Company Historic Site—257 W. 138th St., Harlem. This site was the first office and factory of the Black Swan Record Company, one of the first record companies owned and operated by blacks in America. One of the company's most noted recording artists was Ethel Waters. Black Swan records are now collectors' items.

Canaan Baptist Church—132 W. 166th St., Harlem. (212) 866-0301. With its collection of five spectacular gospel choirs, the Canaan Baptist is well known for its lively and jam-packed Sunday services.

Carver Savings and Loan—75 W. 125th Street, Harlem. Established in 1948 and still in operation, Carver Savings and Loan was the first African-American owned and operated bank in New York State.

Cathedral Church of St. John the Divine—1047 Amsterdam Ave., Harlem. (212) 316-7540. Hours: daily 7a.m.-5p.m. A definite work in progress, the Cathedral of St. John dates back to 1892. Although it remains in operation, a massive remodeling plan is underway that will make the cathedral the world's largest Gothic structure. A popular historic attraction in Harlem, the church is surrounded by 13 acres of greenery with a Biblical garden containing over 100 plants written about in the scriptures. The church sponsors many community activities and performing arts events. The completion of the renovation is expected to take another 75 years.

Children's Art Carnivale—62 Hamilton Terr., Harlem. (212) 234-4093. A non-profit Harlem art school dedicated to the development of the creative spirit where professional artists offer free classes and training programs.

Church of the Intercession and Vicarage—West 155th Street, Harlem. Built in 1911, this is one of Washington Heights' oldest churches. The church's cemetery contains the graves of many notable Harlemites including John James Audubon, founder of the

Audubon Society; Clement Clark Moore, author of "Twas the Night Before Christmas;" John Jacob Astor; and Madame Jumel.

Colonel Young Park—West 143rd to 145th Streets, between Lenox Avenue and Harlem River Drive, Harlem. Named in honor of Colonel Charles Young, one of America's first African-American army officers, this park has served as a center for many of Harlem's baseball and football games. In years past, the Negro Professional Football and Baseball Leagues played here, and now it hosts an annual, city-wide summer basketball program for young people.

Connie's Inn/Shuffle Inn Historic Site—2221 Adam Clayton Powell, Jr., Blvd., Harlem. Originally called the Shuffle Inn in honor of the Sissle and Blake production "Shuffle Along," Connie's Inn was an upscale, basement nightclub established in 1923. It featured an array of major acts including Billie Holiday, Fletcher Henderson, and Zuttie Singleton. One of the three most popular nightspots in Harlem during the late 1920s, Connie's peak period came in 1929 when Louis Armstrong starred in the show "Hot Chocolates." "Ain't Misbehavin'" was one of the famous songs that came out of that show.

Connie's, like most of the other clubs at the time, attracted a fair share of mobsters, and was once the scene of a mob conspired kidnapping. It was also the site of Harlem's famous Tree of Hope which supposedly brought good luck to musicians and actors. In its earliest days as the Shuffle Inn, it employed the then-struggling Fats Waller to work as a delivery boy. Today, Connie's is a commercial storefront.

Cotton Club—See listing in Shopping, Dining & Entertainment section.

Countee Cullen Public Library—104 W. 136th St., Harlem. (212) 491-2070. Hours vary. Part of the New York City Public Library system, Countee Cullen was named after the prominent Harlem Renaissance poet. It is built on the former site of Madame C.J. Walker's home; she was one of the wealthiest, self-made African-

American women of her day. Walker's story is a rags-to-riches legend. The orphaned daughter of poor farmers, Walker invented a hair-straightening product for black women and almost overnight became a millionaire. Her home was designed by the African-American architectural team of Tandy and Foster. Countee Cullen's James Weldon Johnson Reference Collection for Children offers an excellent assortment of books on black life around the world.

Dinah Washington's Residence—345 W. 145h St.,Bowery Bank Building, Harlem. In the early 1960s, singer Dinah Washington lived here in a gorgeous 12th-floor penthouse. Washington, an important blues singer of her time, was often called "Queen of the Blues" because, as Charlie Davis, a former member of her band said, "How many other singers could make a whole band cry?" Most of her major hits were recorded while living here in Harlem, including "What a Difference a Day Makes."

Dizzy Gillespie and Billy Eckstine's Residence—2040 Adam Clayton Powell, Jr., Blvd., near 124th Street, Harlem. This abandoned red building was once an apartment house that served as home for many, many musicians. Billy Eckstine lived here with his wife, as did Dizzy Gillespie and his wife when they were young newlyweds. The two became close friends and often worked on their arrangements together on an old piano. Other well-known residents of 2040 included Clyde Hart, Erroll Garner, Harry Edison, Buck Clayton, and Don Byas.

Duke Ellington's Residence—935 St. Nicholas Ave., near W. 156th St., Harlem. From 1939 to 1961 the great jazz performer resided here in this beautiful Gothic building that has officially been designated a National Historic Landmark. Ellington lived here with his girlfriend, Beatrice Ellis, until the 1960s when they moved downtown. Although Ellis was often called Evie Ellington, the two never married.

While living here, in apartment 4A, Ellington wrote many of his most well-known compositions, performed at the nearby Cotton

Club, and premiered his "Black, Brown, and Beige" which he described as being "parallel to the history of the American Negro," at New York's Carnegie Hall. Ellington died in 1974 and is buried in Woodlawn Cemetery in the Bronx.

Dunbar Apartments—2588 7th Ave., near 149th Street, Harlem. Built in 1926, and financed by John D. Rockefeller, this enormous apartment complex with six buildings and garden courtyards was one of New York's first large cooperatives for African-Americans. Named for the poet and writer Paul Laurence Dunbar, it once served as home for many African-American celebrities and notables including Bill "Bojangles" Robinson, Countee Cullen, W.E.B. DuBois, A. Phillip Randolph, Paul Robeson, and explorer Matthew A. Henson.

Paul Laurence Dunbar is most remembered for his poems and stories in black dialect which portrayed the lives of black people in the rural South. In his book *The Sport of Gods*, Dunbar described the injustices done to a respectable Southern black family, forcing them to move north. The book suggested that however unjust the South may have been, the weak morals and decadent lifestyle in New York City was more dangerous for American blacks. Some of his other books include: *Lyrics and Love and Laughter, Oak and Ivy, Majors and Minors,* and *Folks from Dixie.* Dunbar died in 1906.

Edmond's Historic Site—130th Street and 5th Avenue, Harlem. During the late 1920s and early 1930s, Edmond's was a dingy, basement jazz club patronized by pimps, hookers and gamblers. Most entertainers who performed here exhausted themselves trying to be heard above the din of conversation and the ruffian environment. But it was at Edmond's that singer Ethel Waters began her career. She later described it as "the last stop on the way down." Waters, however, was one of the few performers who could control the crowd. She would stride to the stage, strike a nonchalant pose and wait for silence. Soon after performing at Edmond's, Waters went on to perform at more prominent clubs.

Elmendorf Reformed Church—171 E. 121st St., Harlem. (212)

534-5856. Established in New York City by the Dutch Reformed Church of Holland in 1628, this church has been at its present site for over 200 years. Its congregation is largely made up of West Indian blacks, many from the Dutch Caribbean.

Ethiopian Hebrew Congregation—1 W. 123rd St., Harlem. (212) 534-1058. This synagogue, near Mount Morris Park, has a large congregation of black Jews. New York City's first congregation of black Jews was organized in 1845.

Florence Mills' Residence—220 W. 135th St., Harlem. This house was once the residence of Florence Mills, the theater and singing star who gained acclaim in Europe during the 1920s.

Frank Silvera's Writer's Workshop—317 W. 125th St., 3rd floor, Harlem. (212) 662-8463. Site of a theater once operated by Langston Hughes, the Frank Silvera's Writer's Workshop hosts an annual film festival, a spring concert featuring the Harlem Symphony Orchestra, Sunday afternoon readings, plus dozens of new productions a year. Its main purpose is to develop new playwrights and plays for African-American theater. Pulitzer Prize winner Charles Fuller and playwright Richard Wesley are members.

Fred Johnson Tennis Courts—Adam Clayton Powell, Jr., Boulevard between 150th and 151st Streets, Harlem. Part of the New York City Parks Department, these tennis courts were named after Harlem tennis instructor Fred Johnson. One of Johnson's students was Althea Gibson, America's first black woman tennis champion.

Graham Court Apartments—7th Avenue between 116th and 117th Streets, Harlem. During the Harlem Renaissance, this plush apartment building was one of Harlem's most desirable residences. Built by John J. Astor for upper-class whites in 1901, it was the envy of the neighborhood, complete with an elegantly decorated lobby, 12-foot ceilings, dumbwaiters, arched passageways, and fireplaces. One of the more prominent figures who lived here was the noted black author and folklorist Zora Neale Hurston. Graham Court, however, was not opened to black residents until 1928, and was one of the last large apartment buildings in Harlem to become integrated.

Hamilton Grange—287 Convent Ave., between 141st and 142nd Streets, Harlem. Home of the great American statesman Alexander Hamilton, this Federal-style mansion was moved to this site in 1889. It later served as the chapel for the adjoining St. Luke's Episcopal Church. Donated to the American Scenic and Historical Preservation Society by J.P. Morgan, it is now maintained by the National Park Service.

Hamilton Heights Historic District—West 142nd to 145th Streets between Amsterdam and St. Nicholas Avenues. Originally a part of Alexander Hamilton's estate, the Grange, this peaceful residential neighborhood has an extraordinary variety of architectural styles including grand mansions and simple row houses dating back to the late 1800s.

Harlem River Houses—W. 151st to 153rd Streets near Harlem River Drive. These four-story, red-brick apartment buildings, completed in 1937, were some of the first federally funded and owned housing projects in New York City. They were built as a direct response to the Harlem riots of 1935, and were intended to meet the needs of low-income Harlemites. After protests from the African-American community because the seven-member architectural team appointed to design it had no blacks, black architect John Lewis Wilson was added to the Harlem River Houses' design team. With their landscaped courtyards, decorated with sculptures by African-American artists Richmond Barthe and Paul Manship, the Harlem River Houses once represented a fine quality of life along with a strong sense of community pride. They set a standard for public housing projects across the country in the years that followed their completion.

Harlem School of the Arts—645 St. Nicholas Ave., Harlem. (212) 926-4100. For over 25 years the Harlem School of the Arts has been offering fine quality training in dance, art, music, singing and theater.

Harlem YMCA—180 W. 135th St., Harlem. (212) 281-4100. The Harlem branch of the Young Men's Christian Association, this gathering spot has hosted many notable black artists and entertainers, including Langston Hughes, Ralph Ellison, Claude McKay, Eartha Kitt, Harry Belafonte, Sidney Poitier, and Cicely Tyson. And in 1945, the Harlem Writers' Workshop was founded here.

Holcombe Rucker Memorial Playground—W. 156th to 158th Streets, between Frederick Douglass Boulevard and Harlem River Drive, Harlem. Named in honor of Holcombe Rucker, a Harlemite who sponsored basketball tournaments for disadvantaged youths. Basketball superstar Julius "Dr. J." Irving once practiced on these courts.

Hotel Theresa Historic Site—2090 Adam Clayton Powell, Jr., Blvd., near 125th Street, Harlem. Once Harlem's largest and most famous hotel, the Theresa was a beautiful white-brick lodging that had an assortment of notable characters pass through its doors. Cab Calloway's band often stayed here, even when they were performing at clubs a few hours away in Connecticut. So did Lena Horne, Dizzy Gillespie, Cozy Cole, and Milt Hinton, and most of the celebrities who performed at the nearby Apollo Theater. Lester Young actually lived here before Billie Holiday invited him to move in with her. And it was at the Hotel Theresa that Cab Calloway fired Dizzy Gillespie after he and a few fellow musicians got into trouble for fooling around and throwing spitballs on the stage.

Fortunately, Calloway calmed down, and he and Gillespie made up. In 1958, the funeral of W.C. Handy was held at the Theresa, and a generation later, rock-and-roll guitarist Jimi Hendrix checked in for a few nights.

In addition to musicians and singers, the Hotel Theresa played host to boxer Joe Louis. And in 1960, Cuban Premier Fidel Castro, after checking out of a downtown hotel due to what he considered to be poor treatment, checked into the Hotel Theresa. Castro was in New York to deliver an address to the United Nations, and while staying at the Hotel Theresa was joined by Soviet Union Premier Kruschev. Thousands of spectators and hundreds of policemen gathered at the hotel for the historic event. The Hotel Theresa is now an office building.

Jackie Robinson Park—W. 145th to 155th Streets. Located in the St. Nicholas Historic District, this recreational park with basketball and volleyball courts, an Olympic size swimming pool, bandshell, softball field and play areas, is named in honor of the legendary baseball player. Jackie Robinson was the first African-American to play baseball in the major leagues, and in 1962 was elected to the Baseball Hall of Fame. After he left baseball Robinson became a prominent spokesman and fundraiser for the civil rights movement.

James P. Johnson's Residence—267 W. 140th St., near Frederick Douglass Boulevard. This now run-down building was the home of the great stride piano player James P. Johnson during the early 1920s. Johnson taught Fats Waller to play the piano, and the two of them often practiced together on two pianos in Johnson's home till late in the morning. Johnson shared this apartment with his sister, May Wright Johnson.

James Weldon Johnson's Residence—187 W. 135th Street. From 1925 to 1938, the noted poet, songwriter, lawyer, journalist, diplomat, school principal, civil rights activist, and officer of the NAACP lived here. Born in Jacksonville, Florida, Johnson wrote "Lift Every Voice and Sing," more commonly known as the Negro National Anthem, for schoolchildren to sing at a celebration of the birthday of Abraham Lincoln in 1900. Not long afterward, he moved to New York City with his younger brother, J. Rosamond Johnson, where they formed a highly successful songwriting team with Bob Cole. Johnson believed that an uplifting song would be a way for black people to express their pride in who they were. With the support of the NAACP, he began to encourage the singing of his song as a Negro national anthem. In the years since, it has been sung by millions of black people throughout America. Johnson died in 1938.

Jumel Terrace Historic District—160th to 162nd Streets between St. Nicholas and Edgecombe Avenues, Harlem. This district contains over 20 preserved row houses all erected between 1882 and 1909.

Lafayette Theater Historic Site—7th Avenue between 131st and 132nd Streets, Harlem. Originally built in 1912 to present white plays to white audiences, the Lafayette Theater changed quickly to accommodate the population shift from white to black that occurred in Harlem in the early 1900s. Leased by Lester Walton, a drama critic for the black newspaper New York *Age*, it was transformed into a stock company that was packed with new black talent, and served as a starting point for many black stage performers. Since blacks at that time were not welcome in Broadway theaters, they produced black versions of Broadway plays such as "Dr. Jekyll and Mr. Hyde" at the Lafayette. The Lafayette players also presented shows in which black men and women actually displayed tender, romantic love toward one another, something that could never have been done in a white theater.

In 1913, Leubrie Hill produced the "Darktown Follies" at the Lafayette and revolutionized the standards of musical revues. The show received rave reviews and soon whites were flocking to Harlem to see it. Florenz Ziegfeld purchased a portion of Hill's show and eventually incorporated it into the Ziegfeld Follies.

"Shuffle Along," the first major African-American production to make it to Broadway, was first performed at the Lafayette also in 1913. "Shuffle Along" was followed by "The Chocolate Dandies" and "Blackbirds."

During the 1920s, the Lafayette was one of the two main theaters in Harlem, the other being the Lincoln. The Lafayette, however, was twice the size of the Lincoln and was known throughout the country for its lively revues and variety shows. Located on the main entertainment esplanade of Harlem, the Lafayette hosted all of the major acts that were popular at the time, including Duke Ellington, who made his first New York appearance here as a member of Wilbur Sweatman's band in 1923.

Fats Waller also played at the Lafayette. A story in the New York *Age* on October 1, 1927, reported: "Fats Waller, who has been playing the organ at the Lafayette Theater, was paid a visit by his wife one afternoon. She sat on the same stool with Fats as he was playing. The management objected. Words. Fats quit there and then." The management, of course, insisted that Fats was fired. The Lafayette Theater is now a church.

Langston Hughes' Residence—20 E. 127th St., Harlem. The Harlem Renaissance author and poet, who often portrayed Harlem in his work, lived in this three-story, Italian-style brownstone during the last 20 years of his life. Built in 1869, this ivy-covered building was the only residence Hughes ever occupied for any length of time. The street it is located on is now officially called Langston Hughes Place. Langston Hughes died in 1967.

Lincoln Theater Historic Site—58 W. 135th St., near Lenox Avenue, Harlem. Opened in 1915, the Lincoln Theater was one of Harlem's earliest theaters. Unlike other Harlem clubs, the Lincoln catered to a black audience rather than white. It was at the Lincoln Theater that Fats Waller served as the house organist for years, and a young Count Bassie came to listen. Originally, the Lincoln specialized in serious dramatic productions with a new four-act play every week. In 1915, Scott Joplin fulfilled one of his life dreams when he produced his "Treemonisha" at the Lincoln. The play, the story of an educated young black woman who tries to lead her family away from primitive superstitions, did not sit well with the black audience. Southern plantations and superstitions were too much a part of the recent past of many in the audience and they were not quite ready to accept their folk history as art. Eventually, the Lincoln switched to an all-vaudeville and musical comedy bill. The Lincoln Theater is now a church.

Malcolm Shabazz Masjid (Mosque of Islam)—102 W. 116th St., Harlem. (212) 662-2200. The East Coast headquarters for the Moslem faith, this four-story mosque was named in honor of the late civil rights leader, Malcolm X.

Marcus Garvey Memorial Park—120th to 124th Streets between Madison Avenue and Mount Morris Park West, Harlem. A playground and recreational center with an Olympic size swimming pool and historic fire watchtower built in 1856, this public park was formerly called Mount Morris Park. In 1973 it was renamed in honor of the outspoken black nationalist leader Marcus Garvey, whose movement was headquartered in Harlem. In 1776, the park was the site of a fort defended by George Washington's forces during the Revolutionary War.

Mary Lou Williams' Residence—63 Hamilton Terr., Harlem. This attractive apartment building is where noted jazz pianist Mary Lou Williams lived during the 1940s. It was here that jazz greats Charlie Parker, Thelonious Monk and Dizzy Gillespie came to talk to Williams about their music and show her their new acts.

Metropolitan Baptist Church—151 W. 128th St and Adam Clayton Powell, Jr., Boulevard, Harlem. Registered as a city, state, and national landmark, the Metropolitan Baptist Church, built in 1896, was one of Harlem's earliest black churches.

Minton's Playhouse Historic Site—210 W. 118th St., Cecil Hotel, Harlem. Once a great neighborhood club housed in the Cecil Hotel and run by bandleader Teddy Hill, Minton's Playhouse was known throughout Harlem for its spontaneous informal jazz sessions. In 1941, Minton's house band included Thelonious Monk and Kenney Clarke, who encouraged other jazz performers to jam with them into the early morning hours. Among the other performers who played at Minton's were Charlie Parker, Max Roach, Tadd Dameron and Dizzy Gillespie. Minton's was popular because it was a place where musicians could try out their new acts and explore innovative ways of performing jazz.

Some jazz historians call Minton's the birthplace of the music known as bebop, or bop as it is also called. No one is sure how bop got its name, but most suggest that it came from the vocabulary of nonsense syllables that jazz musicians used in singing jazz phrases such as the scat—do wop de bop—singing that Louis Armstrong first made famous. Others say the name came from the title of Dizzy Gillespie's tune "Bebop." According to Oran Page in "Hear Me Talkin' to Ya," the word bop was coined at Minton's by Fats Waller who would criticize younger musicians' attempts at new sounds by shouting "Stop that crazy boppin' and play that jive like the rest of us." Whatever the derivation, bop came alive at Minton's, as musicians inspired one another and worked together to refine one of the most complex music forms of the jazz era.

These days, the Cecil Hotel offers low-rent housing units for elderly Harlemites, and although Minton's has long been closed, there's talk in the neighborhood about bringing it back to life.

Monroe's Uptown House Historic Site—198 W. 134th St., near Adam Clayton Powell, Jr., Boulevard, Harlem. During the 1930s, Monroe's Uptown House was a major spawning ground for aspiring jazz musicians. Charlie Parker played here as did Billie Holiday. Today, Monroe's is a restaurant.

Morris-Jumel Mansion Museum—Roger Morris Park at W. 160th Street, Harlem. (212) 923-8008. Hours: Tues.-Sun.10a.m.-4p.m. This Georgian-style country mansion, built in 1765 by Roger Morris, served as one of George Washington's headquarters during the Revolutionary War. In 1810 it was bought by Stephen Jumel whose widow married the former vice president of the United States, Aaron Burr, in 1833. It is the only pre-revolutionary house still standing in Manhattan, and houses a collection of historical memorabilia.

Mother A.M.E. Zion Church—140-146 W. 137th St., between Lenox Avenue and Adam Clayton Powell, Jr., Boulevard, Harlem. (212) 234-1545. The first church in New York City organized by and for blacks, Mother A.M.E. Zion was founded in 1796 and

originally built at 156 Church St. with money donated by a former
slave. It was designed by noted African-American architect George
Washington Foster, Jr., and is a magnificent Neo-Gothic structure.

Also known as the "Freedom Church" because of its connection
to the Underground Railroad, the church's famous past members
include Harriet Tubman, Frederick Douglass, Paul Robeson, and a
woman named Isabella who became a legend after announcing
during a Sunday service that she wanted to be called Sojourner
Truth—"Sojourner because I am a wanderer, Truth because God is
truth."

Mount Morris Historic District—W. 119th to 124th Streets, between Mount Morris Park West and Lenox Avenue, Harlem. Developed as a New York suburb following the extension of the rapid
train system in the early 1880s, this historic district includes several
notable churches, simple row houses, and stately townhouses. It also
contains Marcus Garvey Memorial Park.

Museum of the City of New York—5th Avenue at 103rd St.,
Harlem. (212) 534-1672. Hours: Tues.-Sat. 10a.m.-5p.m., Sun.
1-5p.m. A spirited and jam-packed museum dedicated to the history
of New York City. Along with a fine collection of period antiques,
the history of the stock exchange, and a 360-degree diorama of 17th
century New Amsterdam, the museum's permanent collection includes an extensive print and photograph collection on Harlem,
African-American memorabilia such as shoes once belonging to Bill
"Bojangles" Robinson, black theater and music artifacts, paintings
with African-American themes, runaway slave advertisements, and
notes hand-written by Frederick Douglass. The museum also hosts
frequent traveling exhibits on African-American themes.

Our Lady of Lourdes Church—472 W. 142nd St., between Amsterdam and Convent Avenues, Harlem. It was here at Our Lady of
Lourdes that jazz pianist Mary Lou Williams found solace while
depressed and despondent. For about three years she turned away
from music and came here to pray, meditate and help the needy.

Eventually, Williams turned herself around and went back to writing and performing music.

Paul Robeson's Residence—555 Edgecombe Ave., Harlem. This building was the home of noted African-American singer and actor Paul Robeson. Robeson is most remembered for his improvised lyrics to songs such as "Old Man River," his performance in the "Emperor Jones," and the regal dignity he brought to portrayals of African-American characters. Although he was an attorney, Robeson found the discrimination in Harlem law offices to be unbearable, and chose instead to pursue acting. He began his career performing at the Harlem YMCA, and quickly impressed audiences with his sonorous voice, expressive face, and commanding stage presence.

In 1925, he went to London for the production of "The Emperor Jones" and became the first black American dramatic actor to play on the English stage since Ira Aldridge had played Othello over a century earlier. In 1943 Robeson starred in "Othello" himself at New York's Shubert Theater, where the play brought a packed house for 296 consecutive performances.

Following World War II, Robeson publicly criticized the American government for its treatment of black people, and was suspected of wishing to overthrow the government. Although he was neither tried nor convicted of any crime, he was forced to turn over his passport in 1950. Along with not being able to perform abroad, he was blacklisted in the U.S. as well. Eight years later his passport was returned. Later in his life, Robeson was showered with honors and awards in an attempt to make amends for the harsh treatment he had received earlier.

Plantation Club Historic Site—W. 126th Street and Lenox Avenue. An uptown branch of the successful Plantation Club on Broadway and 50th Street, the Plantation Club in Harlem was established in the late 1920s in an attempt to draw away some of the Cotton Club's lucrative business. Cab Calloway had done very well for the Cotton Club, and it was hoped that some of his fans would follow him to the Plantation, just 16 blocks away.

Unfortunately, one night in 1930 the Plantation received a visit from some of New York's most notorious gangsters who proceeded to smash the club to pieces. The club closed and never reopened.

Prince Hall Masonic Lodge—454 W. 155th St., Harlem. (212) 281-2211. This branch of the Masonic Order is named in honor of Prince Hall, an African-American veteran of the Revolutionary War. In the late 1700s, Hall petitioned the Massachusetts legislature to stop the slave trade and establish schools for African-American children.

Renaissance Ballroom Historic Site—150 W. 138th St., Harlem. Next door to the Abyssinian Baptist Church, this two-story red brick building was once a glamorous ballroom and casino. From the 1920s to the 1950s, the Renaissance hosted dance, jazz and cabaret acts including Fletcher Henderson, Lester Young, and Chick Webb.

Riverside Church—Riverside Drive at 122nd Street, Harlem. (212) 222-5900. Established in the 1930s, the Riverside Church has always been known as a multi-cultural and interdenominational place of worship with a very diverse congregation. The church houses the Laura Spellman Rockefeller Carillon, the world's largest with 74 bells. Following services on Sunday, a buffet lunch is served.

St. Andrew's Episcopal Church—2067 5th Ave., at 127th Street, Harlem. Founded in 1829, St. Andrew's has been at this location since 1889. It serves a large predominantly black congregation, many of whom come from the West Indies.

St. Nicholas Historic District—W. 137th to 139th Streets between Adam Clayton Powell, Jr., Boulevard and Frederick Douglass Boulevard. Also known as Strivers Row, this collection of spacious townhouses during the early 1900s served as home to Harlem's most up-and-coming citizens.

St. Phillip's Episcopal Church—240 W. 134th St., Harlem. (212) 862-4940. St. Phillip's was established by slaves and free blacks who broke away from the primarily white congregation of Trinity Episcopal church in lower Manhattan. The building was designed by an African-American architect and constructed on this site in 1918.

Salem Cresent Boxing Club—211 W. 129th St., Harlem. (212) 678-2700. A boxing club dedicated to developing the talent of youngsters, the Salem Cresent Club's former members include boxing champions Sugar Ray Robinson and Sandy Sandler.

Savoy Ballroom Historic Site—Lenox Avenue and 141st Street, Harlem. During the 1920s and '30s, the Savoy Ballroom was the hottest dance hall in Harlem, attracting crowds of up to 5,000 people a night. Its second-story location once covered an entire city block and featured two bandstands and an enormous dance floor. Limousines lined the street outside as well dressed sophisticates made their grand entrances.

It was here that a shy and awkward young girl named Ella Fitzgerald first dazzled audiences with her perfect-pitch voice. Chick Webb, a drummer and bandleader, was known as the "King of the Savoy" and along with his star singer Ella Fitzgerald, his band had top billing at most shows. Competing bands from other cities often challenged Webb and the crowds loved the drama, but Webb usually came out on top. Once, even great swing era band leader Benny Goodman tried to out do Webb, but the crowds let it be known who they favored.

Schomburg Center for Research in Black Culture—515 Lenox Ave., Harlem. (212) 862-4000. Hours: Mon.-Wed. noon-8p.m., Thur.-Sat. 10a.m.-6p.m. A mecca for researchers of African-American culture, the Schomburg is a world renown resource center. Housed in a modern brick and glass building adorned with a stunning sculpture of Othello, the center was founded by Arthur A. Schomburg, a Puerto Rican of African descent who as a child was told that the Negro had no history.

The fascinating collection focuses primarily on the social sciences and humanities and includes an enormous array of books, manuscripts, pamphlets, prints, drawings, paintings, sculpture, photographs, Christmas cards, slavery artifacts, movies, African art and weapons, and civil rights memorabilia. Most are arranged by themes such as Black Artists Working Abroad. There are also special tributes to the Harlem Renaissance and black women. On permanent display are works by Jacob Lawrence and Romare Bearden and four murals painted by Aaron Douglas depicting African-American history from the arrival of slaves to the massive migrations of blacks from the South to the North. The Schomburg also has an extensive music collection including artifacts of ancient tribal instruments, and historic recordings of African-American folk, jazz, and R&B music.

Smalls' Paradise Historic Site—2294 Adam Clayton Powell, Jr., Blvd., at W. 135th Street, Harlem. During Prohibition, Smalls' Paradise was a jumping nightclub where bootleg liquor flowed and patrons dressed in dazzling outfits danced the Charleston. Ed Smalls, the club's original owner, was a descendant of the black Civil War hero Captain Robert Smalls, and he had previously managed the Sugar Cane Club, one of the first Harlem clubs to attract a large white audience.

Opened in 1925 and closed in 1986, Smalls' was originally capable of serving over 1,500 people a night. On Sunday mornings the club featured lavish breakfast dances, and unlike most other Harlem clubs at the time, Smalls' admitted blacks as well as whites. During the war years Smalls' drew big name entertainers such as Benny Goodman and Duke Ellington. In the 1960s it was purchased by basketball player Wilt Chamberlain and became known as Big Wilt's. Today, the club is boarded up and only the memories remain.

Strivers Row—W. 137th to 139th Streets between Adam Clayton Powell, Jr., Boulevard and Frederick Douglass Boulevard. An historic Harlem district that gets its name from the fashionable, proud and successful African-Americans who lived here in the early 1900s and were striving to move up in the world, Strivers Row was originally built in the late 1800s for wealthy white families. The homes, however, fell out of favor because of the lack of public transportation in the area, and by the turn of the century many of these elegant townhouses were purchased by prominent blacks. Some of the well known Harlemites who lived here during the 1920s included Eubie Blake, W.C. Handy, Noble Sissle, and Stepin Fetchit. Reminders of what life was once like here are found in a few signs tacked to the buildings that read "Private road walk your horses." Homes on these tree-lined streets are still considered prominent addresses.

Studio Museum in Harlem—144 W. 125th St., Harlem. (212) 864-4500. Hours: Wed.-Fri. 10a.m.-5p.m., Sat.-Sun. 1-6p.m. Since its opening in 1968, the Studio Museum has come a long way from the small factory loft it once was housed in. It now occupies 60,000 square feet of a five-story building and serves as the centerpiece of New York's African-American art community. Dedicated to the preservation and documentation of the art of black America and the African Diaspora, the museum has a clear sense of purpose with many of the exhibits reflecting on life in Harlem. It houses a permanent collection of works by African-American masters such as Romare Bearden, James VanDerZee, and Jacob Lawrence. It also features shows by emerging artists from various areas around the world, art by Harlem children, and propaganda art. Lectures, seminars, films, concerts, book fairs, tours of artists' studios, lessons on African mask-making and bead work, and story-telling shows are an added bonus.

Sugar Hill—From Edgecombe Avenue to St. Nicholas between 145th and 160th Streets, Harlem. This historic district was one of the most prestigious neighborhoods of Harlem during the 1920s. Some of the noted residents included Duke Ellington, Roy Wilkins, W.E.B. DuBois, Langston Hughes, and Thurgood Marshall.

369th Regiment Armory—2360 5th Ave., between 142nd and 143rd Streets, Harlem. Built between 1921 and 1933, this National Guard armory is the home of the 369th Regiment, also known as the "Harlem Hell Fighters." During World War I, the regiment earned many awards for its outstanding military achievements. It was here, in August of 1960, that a crowd of almost 10,000 Harlemites gathered to listen to Muslim spiritual leader Elijah Muhammad deliver a speech on civil rights and black unity. The structure consists of a drill shed and administration center, and is noted for its combination of medieval and art deco designs.

Tree of Hope Sculpture—131st Street and 7th Avenue. This six-feet high steel structure marks the spot where the original "Tree of Hope" once existed. The Tree of Hope was an actual tree that out-of-work African-American actors and actresses would come to in search of good luck and fortune. The original tree was cut down and replaced by one donated by Bill "Bojangles" Robinson with a bronze plaque that still remains and reads "You wanted a tree of hope and here it is. Best wishes." A piece of the Bojangles tree, which was also cut down, can be found on stage at the Apollo Theater where performers rub it for good luck. In 1972, the abstract red, purple, black and green sculpture was erected on this site.

Trinity Cemetery—153rd to 155th Street at Amsterdam Avenue and Riverside Drive, Harlem. One of the noted graves here is that of John James Audubon, founder of the Audubon Society.

W.E.B. DuBois' Residence—409 Edgecombe Ave., Harlem. This apartment building in Harlem's Sugar Hill district was once the home of scholar and writer W.E.B. DuBois. Renaissance artist Charles Alston also kept an art studio here.

SHOPPING, DINING & ENTERTAINMENT

Afri Art Works Gallery—2033 5th Ave., Harlem. (212) 876-1447. Hours: Mon.-Sat. 10a.m.-7:30p.m. A gallery specializing in paintings, sculpture and crafts from Africa and the Caribbean.

Afri-works—260 W. 125th St., in Mart 125, Harlem. (212) 864-

2236. Hours: daily 10a.m.-6:30p.m. Imported African furniture, lamps, sculpture, Kente cloth, and Egyptian fabrics.

Apollo Theater—253 W. 125th St., Harlem. (212) 749-5838. Likely the most famous landmark in the history of black music in America, this legendary theater has launched hundreds of careers and is still going strong. Almost every major jazz, blues, and R&B performer in the U.S. has performed at the Apollo. Its list of stars include Billie Holiday, Duke Ellington, Louie Armstrong, The Ink Spots, Mahalia Jackson, Count Basie, Sarah Vaughan, Billy Eckstine, Lil Armstrong, Bessie Smith, Ethel Waters, Fats Waller, Pearl Baily, Ray Charles, James Brown, B.B. King, Aretha Franklin, Diana Ross, Wilson Pickett, Smokey Robinson, Al Green, Gladys Knight, Regina Belle, and Michael Jackson.

Legend has it that when a young Elvis Presley first came to New York City the first place he wanted to visit was the Apollo; a similar story is told about the Beatles. Opened in 1914 and originally called the Hurtig & Seamon's New Burlesque Theatre, the Apollo began as a whites-only uptown club known for its bawdy vaudeville shows. In 1935, new owners Frank Schiffman and Leo Brecher took over the theater and did away with the whites-only policy.

Under the new management, the Apollo was transformed into a showplace for aspiring talent and attracted a racially mixed audience. The 2,000-seat, two-balconied theater quickly became famous for its amateur nights during which young ripe performers were subjected to either a very appreciative or a very rude audience. Lena Horne, in her early years, was one of those who had an unfortunate night at the Apollo—the audience booed her performance and threw pennies at the stage.

Although it closed in the late 1970s, Harlem's most important attraction was bought by Percy Sutton, NAACP official and co-founder of Inner City Broadcasting Corporation, in the early 1980s. Sutton paid $250,000 for the abandoned building that was flooded with water and full of rats, then completely renovated the property.

It reopened in 1989 after a multi-million dollar face-lift and is once again in the limelight.

Under Sutton's direction, the Apollo Theater Foundation was formed to secure the heritage and future of the theater. The first Apollo Theater Hall of Fame induction ceremony, a spectacular fundraising event, was held in June of 1993 with more events planned for the future. The Apollo now offers an array of entertainment including the popular amateur nights on Wednesday, comedy acts, rap, R&B, soul, and jazz; it houses a permanent exhibit of memorabilia of the theater's early history.

Asmara Restaurant—951 Amsterdam Ave., Harlem. Lunch and dinner. Although known for its authentic Ethiopian cuisine, Asmara also offers American and Italian dishes prepared Ethiopian-style. Specialties include: tibesi beef and peppers, injera bread, vegetarian and grain dishes.

Baobab Tree Gallery—1439 Amsterdam Ave., at 132nd Street, Harlem. (212) 926-0027. Hours: Mon.-Sat. noon-9p.m., Sun. 2-6p.m. Imported African sculptures, woodcarvings, jewelry, leather crafts, and shoes.

Boys Choir of Harlem—(212) 749-1717. The internationally acclaimed choir offers a variety of performances throughout the year at various locations, including works by Duke Ellington, Bach, Vivaldi, and popular music.

Copeland's Restaurant—549 W. 145th St., Harlem. (212) 234-2356. Lunch and dinner. A Harlem favorite since the 1960s, Copeland's packs them in each Sunday for a Southern-style, all-you-can-eat brunch with live harp music in the background. Near the entrance is a display about famous people and their favorite meals, such as Dizzy Gillespie's love of peanut soup and Ossie Davis' penchant for oxtails. The menu includes Cajun and Southern specialties: crab cakes, Louisiana gumbo, shrimp etoufee, barbecued ribs, and sweet potato pie. Reservations suggested. Plans are in the works for the 1994 opening of Copeland's Country Kitchen, a larger version of the original at 125th Street and 7th Avenue.

Cotton Club—666 W. 125th St., Harlem. (212) 663-7980. Hours vary, closed Tuesday. Harlem's dazzling and world renown speakeasy, the Cotton Club during the 1920s catered to a high-society whites-only clientele. Run by some of New York's most notorious gangsters, it was a bastion of glamorous contradiction and the perfect symbol of its era—a time when whites invaded the "capital of black America" to drink prohibition beer, rub elbows with the mob, and be entertained by the fabled "New Negro" entertainers.

In its heyday, the Cotton Club was a hot and sultry place where Duke Ellington, Cab Calloway, Louis Armstrong, Bill "Bojangles" Robinson, and Ethel Waters all left their mark. Its "high-yaller" chorus girls were the talk of the town, attracting curious audiences from around the world who just had to stop in for a show. The Columbia Broadcasting System broadcasted live from the Cotton Club and jazz lovers across the country tuned in to the robust sounds of the Cotton Club Orchestra.

When Prohibition was repealed and the Depression set in, Harlem's breadlines became too painful for the audiences to bare, and the Cotton Club fell into hard times. Originally located on Lenox Avenue, the Cotton Club moved to W. 48th Street in 1936 and carried on for a few more years. By the 1950s, both of the Cotton Clubs had been torn down, and all that remained was the memory of better days. But in 1978, a modern version of the old legend was opened at its present 125th Street location. The new club and restaurant features an ever-changing line-up of performers including live blues, jazz and comedy acts, and a weekend gospel brunch.

Dance Theater of Harlem—466 W. 152 St., Harlem. (212) 690-2800. Founded by Arthur Mitchell, one of the few black male ballet dancers credited with transcending the color line, the Dance Theater of Harlem is America's first successful all-black ballet company.

A graduate of New York's High School of the Performing Arts, Mitchell as a young man studied with the School of American Ballet, the educational arm of the New York City Ballet. At the time, Mitchell experienced the racism that had kept many other black male dancers out of the field—white parents objected to his taking classes with their daughters. But Mitchell graduated from the school and in 1955 joined the prestigious company working under the direction of George Balanchine.

Although he gained acclaim through his appearances with the New York City Ballet, Mitchell's career was not without controversy. The company received letters complaining about his interracial duets, and television producers tried to prevent him from appearing in broadcasted productions. Balanchine stood up for Mitchell, and told the critics that if Mitchell was not allowed to dance, the New York City Ballet would not perform.

By the late 1960s, Mitchell was involved in setting up ballet companies in other parts of the world. The idea for his all-black Dance Theater of Harlem came to him in 1968 on the day Dr. Martin Luther King, Jr., was assassinated. Mitchell decided that he needed to create an all-black company along with a school so that young black dancers would have a better opportunity to break into the world of classic dance.

Despite its name, the Dance Theater of Harlem began operations in a loft in Greenwich Village in 1969, and eventually moved uptown to Harlem a few years later. By 1976, the school had 1,300 students, and the company 27 dancers. With each passing year, the company has gained greater recognition in the U.S. and abroad, and has been able to mount ambitious productions such as "Swan Lake," "Giselle," "Fancy Free," and "Phoenix Rising." These days, still under the direction of Mitchell, the company tours for up to 30 weeks each year, and when not on tour, performs at various theaters in New York each spring.

Dar'thard Creations & Collectibles—260 W. 125th St., in Mart 125, Harlem. (212) 932-1632. Hours: daily 10a.m.-6p.m. A hand-crafted jewelry boutique with African designs, such as gold and silver Yoruba earrings, amber necklaces, and crocheted ear lace earrings.

Forces of Nature Dance Company—14 Mt. Morris Park W., Harlem. (212) 289-2705. A vivacious dance company with an ecclectic repertoire including African, modern, and folkloric dances. Various locations and times.

Grinnel Gallery—800 Riverside Dr. at 158th Street, Harlem. (212) 927-7941. By appointment only. A fine art gallery featuring works for sale by African-American and Caribbean painters, sculptors, and photographers.

H.A.D.L.E.Y. Players—207 W. 133rd St., Harlem. (212) 862-1179. The Harlem Artist Development League Especially For You, H.A.D.L.E.Y. Players is a theater group founded by Gertrude Jeanette. It presents four major family entertainment plays a year from October through June in the basement of the St. Phillip's Church. The plays, ranging from comedies to dramas and musicals, are usually by African-American playwrights and have a mixed cast of performers.

Harlem Restoration Thrift Shop—461 W. 125th St., Harlem. (212) 864-6992. Hours: Mon.-Fri. 9:30a.m.-4:30p.m. A genuine, second-hand shop run by the Harlem Renaissance Restoration Project with profits donated to the project.

Harlem Street Gallery—121 W. 125th St., Harlem. (212) 866-0283. Hours: Mon.-Thur. 1-6p.m. At the corner of Lenox Avenue, the Harlem Street Gallery is an outdoor gallery that sells inexpensive prints and posters relating to African-American culture.

Jamaican Hot Pot Restaurant—2260 Adam Clayton Powell, Jr., Blvd., Harlem. (212) 491-5270. Lunch and dinner. A small eatery with friendly service and some of the best Jamaican cooking this side of Montego Bay. Menu favorites include: curried goat, baby oxtails in brown gravy, ackee and salt fish, collard greens, jerk chicken, fried plantains, and homemade fruit punch.

La Famille Restaurant—2017 5th Ave., at 125th Street, Harlem. (212) 722-9806. Lunch and dinner. A friendly, family eatery with live music on weekends that has been hosting some of the liveliest and most varied jam sessions in the city for over ten years. Authentic, Southern-style meals include: shell steak, baked Virginia ham, short ribs, macaroni and cheese, candied yams, collard greens, black-eyed peas, and deep dish peach cobbler. Live music Wednesday through Sunday.

LaRocque Bey School of Dance and Drumming—180 W. 135th St. in the YMCA building, Harlem. (212) 926-0188. One of the finest Afro-Caribbean dance troupes in the country, LaRocque Bey offers performances throughout the year focusing on the history and culture of blacks in America and the Caribbean. It also offers African dance classes and exercise instruction with African drum music.

Liberation Book Shop—421 Lenox Ave., at 131st Street, Harlem. (212) 281-4615. Hours: Tues.-Sat. 11a.m.-6p.m. A bookstore and neighborhood gathering spot with one of the largest selections of African-American, African and Caribbean books in New York City.

Mart 125—260 W. 125th St., Harlem. A massive, multi-cultural shopping center with over 50 African and African-American specialty shops that sell African art, jewelry, clothing, foods, records and tapes, and books. Shop hours vary.

National Black Theater—5th Avenue at 125th St., Harlem. (212) 497-5615. A multi-cultural theater company based on the traditions of African and West Indian drama and dance, the National Black Theater was one of the most revolutionary theater groups to arise during the 1960s. Founded by Barbara Ann Teer, a Broadway actress, the theater started as a small hands-on company with lighting and sound technicians dancing in the chorus. The NBT's goal was and still is to entertain as well as raise community consciousness about African-American culture. Originally, the actors in the company called themselves liberators and during intermissions they mingled with the audience and the plays were called rituals or revivals.

Today the NBT is housed in a $5.6 million, state-of-the-art

288-seat arena that has some of the finest examples of African art including copper relief work and carved totems. The theater still encourages audience participation and feedback, and showcases the works of African-American writers, directors and actors. Recent productions have included the award-winning plays "Fruits of Miss Morning," "The Legacy," and "Doo Wop Love."

Opera Ebony—(212) 977-2110. In residence at Aaron Davis Hall of City College, Opera Ebony is dedicated to creating opportunities for African-American opera singers, composers, and conductors. Founded in 1974, the company performs an array of works by African-American composers, along with classical works of music. Its schedule varies.

Rainbow Music Shop—102 W. 125th St., Harlem. (212) 864-5262. A fabulous selection of blues, jazz, R&B and gospel records and tapes.

Showman's Cafe—2321 Frederick Douglass Blvd., near 125th Street, Harlem. (212) 864-8941. Formerly located next door to the Apollo, Showman's is one of the few authentic jazz clubs remaining in Harlem. During its early days, jazz greats such as Lionel Hampton, Count Bassie, Dizzy Gillespie and Nat King Cole used to stop in for a drink. A simple and friendly club, Showman's still features terrific live jazz, and along with its staple of neighborhood regulars, attracts busloads of Japanese and European tourists. The atmosphere is down-home and cozy, with young and old, rich and poor, all gathering for a good time. Live music Thursday through Sunday and Southern-style food.

Sylvia's Restaurant—328 Lenox Ave., at 126th St., Harlem. (212) 996-0660. Breakfast, lunch and dinner. The so-called "Harlem Queen of Soul Food," Sylvia Woods is definitely a neighborhood character and her restaurant a veritable institution. Born in South Carolina, Woods worked in a factory before spending eight years as a luncheonette waitress in New York. In 1962 she bought this restaurant which became Sylvia's and during the past 30 years expanded it from a tiny counter with four booths to a large establishment with three dining rooms. Woods, however, still oversees what goes on in the kitchen.

This simple and friendly place is often packed with both locals and tourists from around the world. Filmmaker Spike Lee, a frequent customer, shot a scene for his film "Jungle Fever" at Sylvia's. Along with her standard fare, Sylvia offers daily specials including: chitlins, chicken and dumplings, eggs and salmon cakes, smothered pork chops, collard greens, candied yams, barbecue ribs, and corn bread.

Twenty-Two West Restaurant—22 W. 135th St., between Lenox and Fifth Avenues, Harlem. (212) 862-7770. Breakfast, lunch and dinner. An informal soul food eatery with a terrific selection of hamhocks, oxtails, chicken livers, fried chicken, and biscuits.

Wilson's Restaurant and Bakery—1980 Amsterdam Ave., at 158th St., Harlem. (212) 923-9821. Breakfast, lunch and dinner. A popular and very busy locals' eatery and bakery with good service. Inexpensive, Southern-style classics include: chicken and waffles, cheese eggs, grits, smothered steak, mashed sweet potatoes, pigs feet, fried chicken, collard greens, macaroni and cheese, charbroiled lamb chops, corn muffins, biscuits, sweet potato pie, and coconut cake. Reservations suggested on Sunday.

Zula Cafe—1260 Amsterdam Ave., at 122nd St., Harlem. (212) 663-1670. Lunch and dinner. A lively East African eatery that attracts many African students, so the food must be authentic. Served family style, the meals are light and healthy. Specialties include: lentil and chick pea dishes, chicken in a tomato/jalepeno sauce, lamb and peppers, and Ethiopian honey wine.

Harlem Opera House, around 1906.

The famous Cotton Club when Bill Robinson and Cab Calloway were on the program.

The Salvation Army stationed outside the Cotton Club in 1937.

A copy of the Cotton Club program now in the Lincoln Center Library.

Elegantly gowned chorus line on stage at the Cotton Club.

Billie Holiday brought down the house with her blues singing.

Charlie Parker in 1953, two years before his death at age 34.

The Savoy, at the corner of 140th Street and Lenox, as it appeared in 1948.

The Hotel Theresa, once Harlem's largest and most famous hotel.

Line for the Apollo Theater, top left corner, goes down the block and around the corner.

Ray Charles and Bill Crosby at the Apollo.

B.B. King with Eric Clapton at the Apollo Theater.

Diana Ross at the Apollo.

Ross joined by Congressman Charles Rawgel and Percey Sutton at the Apollo.

Sylvia Woods, owner of Sylvia's restaurant in Harlem.

The Boys Choir of Harlem.

Renee Robinson in Alvin Ailey's Cry.

The Company in Alvin Ailey's The Mooche.

The future of Metropolitan Baptist Church, Harlem.

Strivers Row, an historic neighborhood in Harlem.

The Blue Note, first-rate for mainstream jazz.

Chapter 3

The Bronx

*A*lthough surrounded by water on three sides, the Bronx is the only borough that is topographically attached to the New York mainland. Scarred by images of abandoned buildings, piles of rubble, rampant crime and urban ugliness that have punctuated news reports for the past 20 years, the Bronx, to the surprise of many, has some serene pockets of suburban mansions with hilly, green lawns, and the saving grace of over 5,000 acres of public parks that make up almost one-fourth of its total area as well. It is also home to the first-rate Bronx Zoo, Yankee Stadium, Edgar Allen Poe's cottage, Orchard Beach, and the infamous Bronx cheer. In 1639 the Dutch West India Company purchased the land then called Kreskekeck from Native Indians. Five years later a Scandinavian named Jonas Bronck bought 500 acres and turned it into his family's homestead. Soon after, the area became known as the Broncks. Throughout the mid-1600s, more settlers came, but a series of Indian uprisings discouraged development. During the 1700s, some of the settlers imported African slaves to work the land and maintain their homes. A glimpse of what early Bronx life was like for these slaves can be found at the Van Cortlandt House Museum, where a special African-American history tour portrays the slaves' perspective.

Until the mid-1800s, the Bronx remained a peaceful rural settlement inhabited by a few landowners and farmers with a population of less than 5,000. The late 1880s brought the Third Avenue Elevated Railway to the Bronx, and a few years later European immigrants began settling in the borough. In 1900 the population soared to 200,000.

Throughout the next four decades, the Bronx became a haven for working-class immigrants—Irish, Italians and Jews—who established ethnic enclaves throughout the borough. Following World War II, tons of landfill—a New York euphemism for garbage—were dumped onto the eastern marshland sections of the Bronx in order to create more residential areas.

Eventually, many of the European immigrants were able to work their way up in status, and abandon their Bronx apartment buildings for more suburban neighborhoods in Westchester and Long Island. From the 1940s through the 1960s, as many whites left the borough, more and more African-Americans and Puerto Ricans began moving into the Bronx, and today they represent a substantial percentage of the borough's 1.2 million residents. The 1970s brought hard-times and inner-city nightmares for many of the Bronx's dense low-income neighborhoods. In 1978 President Carter paid a visit to the South Bronx and declared it a national symbol of urban decay that had to be addressed. Immediately after, he proposed a federally funded revitalization project for the area. Today, the Bronx is marked by extreme contrasts. Neighborhoods such as Riverdale, City Island and Pelham Bay Park are comfortable, safe and well-maintained. In the South and Central Bronx, dilapidated tenements, vandalism and crime remain the norm. Since the African-American population in the Bronx is a relatively recent phenomenon, the borough doesn't have a great deal of African-American history. It does, however, have Woodlawn cemetery, where a stroll along the peaceful lanes serves as an eery history lesson on jazz musicians. There, beneath the towering oak trees, lie the graves of many great performers including W.C. Handy, Duke Ellington, and Miles Davis.

HISTORIC SITES AND CULTURAL CENTERS

Billie Holiday's Gravesite—The new St. Raymond's Cemetery, 177th Street and Lafayette Avenue, the Bronx. (718) 792-1133. The noted blues singer, who died on July 17, 1959, is buried here beside her mother Sadie, in the St. Paul's section, range 56, plot 29.

Bright Temple African Methodist Episcopal Church—812 Faile St., Hunts Point, the Bronx. (718) 542-7777. Built in 1860, this Gothic Revival structure was once a luxurious mansion known as Sunnyslope. It now houses the Bright Temple AME Church and has a predominantly African-American congregation. Services on Sunday.

Bronx Museum of the Arts—1040 Grand Concourse, the Bronx. (718) 681-6000. Hours: Sat.-Thur. 10a.m.-4p.m., Sun. 11a.m.-4:30p.m. Founded in 1971 as part of a community effort to revitalize the borough, the Bronx Museum of the Arts is dedicated to serving its multicultural community. Along with contemporary art exhibits, including a good collection of works by Romare Bearden, the Bronx Museum occasionally offers rotating exhibits on African and African-American art. Past shows have included Hidden Heritage: Afro-American Art, 1800-1950; and Devastation/Resurrection: The South Bronx.

Gallery 69—69 Bruckner Blvd., the Bronx. (718) 665-8132. Hours: Wed.-Sun. 11a.m.-6p.m. A gallery specializing in paintings, sculpture, and textiles by artists from Africa, the Caribbean, North and South America.

Van Cortlandt House Museum—246th Street and Broadway, inside Van Cortlandt Park, the Bronx. (718) 543-3344. Hours: Tues.-Fri. 10a.m.-3p.m., Sat.-Sun. 11a.m.-4p.m. Located in the north-central Bronx, this colonial-style mansion was built in 1748 by Frederic Van Cortlandt, a descendant of the wealthy Van Cortlandt family associated with the Dutch West India Company. In

1783, George Washington maintained his headquarters in the house just before he launched his campaign to recapture New York from the British. Furnished with English, Dutch and Colonial antiques, the mansion reveals what life in the 18th century was like for both the wealthy residents and the slaves who worked the property. During the late 1700s and early 1800s, about 17 slaves lived at Van Cortlandt and their duties included tending crops and livestock, spinning flax, weaving cloth, candle-making, soap-making, and carving furniture. Records reveal that one slave, a man named Piero, was a skilled craftsman who married and lived with his family on the property. In addition to the regular tour of the house offered by the museum, a special "African-American Life at Van Cortlandt" tour is available during Black History Month in February and by special appointment. This tour takes an unusual approach featuring two walk-throughs of the home. The first is a view of the house from the slave perspective including inspections of the cooking areas, laundry room, and wheat plantation that once surrounded the house. The second looks at how it felt to live in the house and be served by the slaves. The African-American tour also takes visitors up to a small third-floor chamber that served as the sleeping quarters for the slaves.

Woodlawn Cemetery—Webster Avenue and 233rd Street, the Bronx. (718) 920-0500. Dating back to the Civil War, Woodlawn Cemetery is a pastoral stretch of land with rolling hills, old shade trees, and a deep blue lake. A stroll through the grounds, although a bit morbid, offers a walking history lesson loaded with jazz memories.

Among the many notable graves is the family plot of Duke Ellington, adorned with simple stone markers and two stone crosses. Nearby, under two imposing trees, is the grave of jazz trumpeter Miles Davis. Davis' tomb, a slab of shiny black granite, reads "In Memory of Sir Miles Davis," the title bestowed upon him by the Knights of Malta. The fact that the two jazz greats are buried so close to each other, cemetery officials say, was just a coincidence.

Cootie Williams, a trumpeter in Ellington's orchestra; Joe "King"

Oliver, a cornetist who led the Creole Jazz Band; and W.C. Handy, the "father of the blues," are also buried at Woodlawn, as is the famed nightclub owner Bricktop. All of them are buried in marked graves except for Oliver, who died penniless and is buried in an unmarked plot in the Salvia section.

Chapter 4

Brooklyn

At the southwestern tip of Long Island, Brooklyn is New York's most populous borough, boasting over 2.3 million residents, many of whom are marked by that pungent in-your-face accent mockingly referred to as Brooklynese. As a community, it has one of New York's strongest identities, far greater than that of Queens or the Bronx. Primarily a residential area, Brooklyn's 78 square miles include high dry bluffs, a tacky but lovable beachfront boardwalk, the dramatically beautiful Brooklyn Bridge, and the second largest African-American community in the United States. Established by the Dutch in the early 1600s and originally called Breuckelen, Brooklyn throughout the 16-1700s consisted of several small farming communities that imported African slaves via the West Indies to work the land. By the late 1700s, almost a quarter of the population consisted of slaves. When an outbreak of yellow fever in Manhattan during the 1790s caused many residents to desert the island in search of a healthier place to live, the overall population of Brooklyn swelled.

In the early 1800s, two distinct African-American communities took root in Brooklyn. Weeksville, inside what is now the area of Bedford-Stuyvesant, was established in the 1830s and named after one of its first black landowners, John Weeks. About a mile away, a sister community known as Carrville was established a few years later by William Thomas, an African-American chimney sweep from

Brooklyn

Manhattan who purchased 30 acres of woodlands and then sold parcels to other black investors.

By the late 1870s, the two communities had about 700 black residents, most of whom worked as laborers, seamen, sailmakers, carpenters and cooks. For the most part, Weeksville and Carrville remained independent from the white communities in Brooklyn by maintaining their own schools, churches, orphanages, old-age homes and cemeteries. During the 1863 draft riots many blacks fled Manhattan for the safety and refuge of Weeksville, where residents placed a 24-hour guard around the settlement as a defense against the attacking white mobs; and in 1865, the African Civilization Society, an organization that helped freed slaves, established its headquarters there. About a decade later, the Brooklyn community of Fort Green began to develop its own substantial African-American community.

During the late 1890s, an increase in urban growth throughout New York City brought large numbers of whites to the areas surrounding Weeksville and Carrville. Slowly but steadily the new residents pushed the blacks out of their communities, and by the 1920s both Weeksville and Carrville slipped into obscurity. After the 1920s, however, as Harlem began to lose its appeal, a large number of African-Americans began settling in Bedford-Stuyvesant, and by 1940, the black population reached 65,000. It was in the neighborhood of Bedford-Stuyvesant that Shirley Chisholm, the first black congresswoman, was born.

Throughout the 1940s, the Brooklyn neighborhood of Flatbush welcomed thousands of West Indian immigrants who established their own bustling network of small businesses. Today, the West Indian population in Brooklyn is quite large and each Labor Day weekend several hundred thousand West Indians and African-Americans gather for an enormous Caribbean-style carnival that snakes its way along Eastern Parkway.

The 1960s and early 1970s were not the best of times for Brooklyn's African-American neighborhoods. Most were troubled with high-unemployment, crime, and brutally violent race riots. But fortunately, during the late 1970s and early 1980s, many underwent a period of renovation and gentrification that mended the communities and restored hope for the residents.

Today, several of Brooklyn's African-American neighborhoods are full of civic pride and a strong Afrocentric spirit. The African-American community in Fort Green is a trendy enclave of artists, musicians, and writers. Home-base for many of New York's "new black elite," Fort Green is often called America's "Happening 'Hood." The Brooklyn Arts Council has helped the borough keep its African-American heritage alive by sponsoring various cultural events that relate to African-American, African, and West Indian cultures. And even a few remnants of the historic community of Weeksville have been brought back to life by a group of dedicated preservationists who are determined not to let their history be forgotten.

HISTORIC SITES AND CULTURAL CENTERS

Al-Karim School—221 Kingston Ave., Brooklyn. (718) 756-0333. A privately run, accredited elementary and junior-high school that places an emphasis on African-American history and culture.

Arthur Ashe Memorial Tree—Society of the Preservation of Weeksville and Bedford-Stuyvesant, 1698 Bergen St., Brooklyn. In 1993, the New York Department of Parks and Recreation dedicated this sweet gum tree in honor of the Tennis Hall of Famer and civil rights advocate Arthur Ashe. Ashe, the first black male to win the U.S. Open and Wimbledon, died in 1993.

Bedford-Stuyvesant—Bounded by Myrtal Avenue to the north, Eastern Parkway to the south, Classon Avenue to the west, and Broadway to the east. This triangular shaped neighborhood known as Bed-Stuy is home to one of the largest African-American communities in the United States. Originally two separate communities–

Bedford, a Dutch settlement established in 1663, and Stuyvesant, a posh upper middle-class neighborhood established in the 1890s –the combined name came about in the 1930s after the "Brooklyn Eagle" newspaper reported incidents of racial conflicts between the blacks who lived in Bedford and the whites who lived in Stuyvesant. Throughout the 1930s and '40s, Bedford-Stuyvesant attracted many rural Southern blacks as well as West Indian immigrants who settled in the neighborhood.

Today, the Bed-Stuy African-American community is the second largest in the country after Chicago's South Side. In recent years, many young black professionals have moved into the area and parts of the neighborhood are in the midst of an urban renaissance. Although inner-city decay is prevalent, Bed-Stuy is also full of beautiful tree-lined streets with restored, historic brownstones. Each July, the community hosts a week-long African Street Festival with hundreds of street vendors and entertainment by both Africans and African-Americans.

Bethany Baptist Church—460 Sumner Ave., Bedford-Stuyvesant, Brooklyn. (718) 455-8400. Founded during the early 1900s, the Bethany Baptist Church was one of the first black churches established in Bedford-Stuyvesant during the great northward migration of rural blacks from the South.

Boys and Girls High School—1700 Fulton Ave., Bedford-Stuyvesant, Brooklyn. (718) 467-1700. The largest school in the neighborhood, Boys and Girls sponsors many cultural events including the annual African Street Festival in July. The school's exterior is adorned with a dramatic mural depicting African-American history, from slavery to the present, painted by Ernest Crichlow. In 1990, Nelson Mandela made an appearance here during his three-day visit to New York City.

Bridge Street African Methodist Episcopal Church—273 Stuyvesant Ave., Bedford-Stuyvesant, Brooklyn. (718) 452-3936. Founded in 1818, the Bridge Street AME Church once served as a stop on the

Underground Railroad, and is the oldest African-American church in Brooklyn.

Brooklyn Museum—200 Eastern Pkwy., Brooklyn. (718) 638-5000. Hours: Tue.-Sat. 10a.m.-5p.m. A stately marble column museum with five floors of exhibit space, the Brooklyn Museum in 1923 became the first museum in the United States to exhibit African art objects as works of art rather than as artifacts. Although enormous in size, the museum is very accessible and a pleasure to explore. Included in the collection are excellent exhibits on Egypt and Africa; a large collection of works by African-American artists Jacob Lawrence, Richard Mayhew, and Ernest Crichlow; and rotating exhibits on the African-American experience.

Charles Moore Center for Ethnic Studies—357 Jay St., Brooklyn. (718) 469-8211. A multi-cultural educational center where children can learn about African heritage through dance. Recitals for the public are held several times a year.

Concord Baptist Church—833 Marcy Ave., Bedford-Stuyvesant, Brooklyn. (718) 622-1818. Founded in 1848, the Concord Baptist Church was built by the early African-American residents of Brooklyn and now has one of the largest black congregations in the country with over 12,000 members.

Fort Green—Bounded by the Brooklyn Navy Yard to the north, Atlantic Avenue to the south, Clinton Avenue to the east, and Flatbush Avenue to the west. This gritty yet gracious neighborhood, during the late 1800s and early 1900s, contained about a third of Brooklyn's black population and was known as "Brooklyn's Black Belt." Although originally an elite enclave populated by upper-middle-class whites, Fort Green has long had a substantial middle-class black presence. Following the Depression, the area declined and many of the once beautiful brownstones adorned with wrought-iron fences were turned into rooming houses.

During the late 1970s, Fort Green underwent a massive renovation and once again became a desirable neighborhood. This time around, many young black professionals moved in to the area, transforming it into a bastion of black middle-class. Today, Fort Green is a lively place that *Essence* magazine has termed the "Happening 'Hood." About 70 percent of its 54,000 residents are black, and many musicians, artists and filmmakers now call it home. Along with long-time black residents such as jazz singer Betty Carter and painter Ernest Crichlow, the Fort Green community now includes trumpeter Terence Blanchard, film director Ernest R. Dickerson, and actress Lonette McKee. It also serves as the headquarters for 40 Acres and a Mule, the film company owned by Spike Lee. Lee, a neighborhood regular, is often called "the mayor."

Hanson Place Seventh Day Adventist Church—88 Hanson Pl., Fort Green, Brooklyn. (718) 783-9354. This monumental Greek Revival church, built in the 1850s, served as a station on the Underground Railroad. Services are held on Sunday.

Howard Colored Orphan Asylum Historic Site—Troy Avenue and Dean Street, Weeksville, Brooklyn. During the late 1800s, this three-story brick building housed orphaned African-American children whose parents had either died or worked as domestics following the abolition of slavery. Founded in 1866 by Mrs. S.A. Tillman, a black woman who also sheltered many children in her Manhattan home, the orphanage moved to Long Island in 1911, and after years of hardship, closed following World War I. It was named in honor of General O.O. Howard, Commissioner of the United States Freedman's Bureau.

Institutional Church of God in Christ—170 Adelphi St., between Myrtle and Willoughby Avenues, Brooklyn. (718) 625-9175. The main draw of this church is its 50-member Institutional Radio Choir, a gospel group that along with performing regularly at the church on Sunday mornings, starred in the Broadway show "Gospel at Colonus," and broadcasts Sunday evening on radio station WWRL 1600 AM.

Jackie Robinson's Residence—5224 Tilden St., Brooklyn. Not open to the public. This was the long-time Brooklyn home of John Roosevelt "Jackie" Robinson, who in the mid-1940s opened doors for other African-American athletes by becoming the first black baseball player to be accepted into the major leagues.

Lefferts Homestead—Flatbush Avenue and Empire Boulevard, in the eastern corner of Prospect Park, Brooklyn. (718) 965-6505. Hours: Sat.-Sun noon-4p.m. Built between 1777 and 1783, this two-story, eight-room house was recently restored and turned into a museum. Along with providing insight into an 18th century plantation homestead, it offers a glimpse of what life was like for the several slaves who lived and worked on the property.

Magnolia Tree Earth Center & George Washington Carver Gallery—679 Lafayette Ave., Bedford-Stuyvesant, Brooklyn. (718) 387-2116. Hours: Mon.-Thur. and Sat. 10a.m.-5p.m. Established in 1972, this environmental education center is committed to improving the quality of life in African-American communities. Its famous magnolia tree, transplanted from North Carolina, is one of two trees in New York City officially designated as a landmark. The center's George Washington Carver Gallery offers a variety of exhibits throughout the year.

Medgar Evers College—1650 Bedford Ave., Bedford-Stuyvesant, Brooklyn. (718) 270-4991. Named in honor of the Mississippi-born civil rights leader who fought for desegregation, Medgar Evers College is the only African-American oriented college in the City University of New York system. Medgar Evers was assassinated in 1963 and his death prompted President Kennedy to send a civil rights bill to Congress that called for guaranteed equal access to public places.

Plymouth Congregational Church—1223 E. 96th St., Brooklyn. (718) 649-5962. During the Civil War, this church served as a station on the Underground Railroad, and Henry Ward Beecher preached to the congregation about the importance of the abolitionist movement. Beecher's sister, Harriet Beecher Stowe, was the author of "Uncle Tom's Cabin."

St. Phillips Church Historic Site—Dean Street between Troy and Schnectady Avenues, Weeksville, Brooklyn. The St. Phillips Church, formerly at this location, was the site in 1907 of the founding of the first Black Community Company of the United Boys Brigade of America, the forerunner of the Boy Scouts of America.

Siloam Presbyterian Church—260 Jefferson Ave., Bedford-Stuyvesant, Brooklyn. (718) 789-7050. This pre-Civil War church once served as one of the several stops on the Underground Railroad in Brooklyn. Services are held on Sunday.

Simmons African Arts Museum—1063 Fulton St., Bedford-Stuyvesant, Brooklyn. (718) 230-0933. Hours: Sat.-Sun. noon-6p.m. A privately owned viewing gallery that features an ecclectic collection of contemporary African art from 12 West African countries including masks, sculptures and paintings.

Society for the Preservation of Weeksville and Bedford-Stuyvesant—1698 Bergen St., Bedford-Stuyvesant, Brooklyn. (718) 756-5250. Hours: Mon.-Fri. 9a.m.-5p.m. The Society for the Preservation of Weeksville and Bedford-Stuyvesant is dedicated to preserving the African-American history of these two communities. It maintains a small museum and sponsors traveling exhibits, educational events, festivals, and walking tours of the neighborhood.

Washington Temple Church of God in Christ—1372 Bedford Ave., Bedford-Stuyvesant, Brooklyn. (718) 789-7545. With seven resident choir groups, the Washington Temple Church is known throughout Brooklyn for its jubilant Sunday gospel services with keyboard and percussion instruments.

Weeksville Historic District—Bordered by Troy Avenue, Ralph Avenue, Fulton Street and E. New York Avenue. Established in the late 1830s as a community by and for free blacks, Weeksville was a lively African-American neighborhood until the late 1890s. Some of the noted early residents included Major Martin Delaney, a grandson of an enslaved West African prince who worked as a journalist for the Weeksville newspaper and helped hundreds of escaped slaves find freedom through the Underground Railroad; Moses R. Cobb, one of Brooklyn's first black policemen and a former slave who walked from North Carolina to New York City; and Dr. Susan Smith McKinney-Steward, one of the earliest black female doctors in the United States born in Weeksville in 1847. When she died in 1918, Dr. McKinney-Steward was eulogized by W.E.B. Dubois. During its heyday, Weeksville had its own churches, schools, orphanage, old-age home, and cemetery.

Weeksville Hunterfly Road Houses—1698-1708 Bergen St., between Rochester and Buffalo Roads. (718) 756-5250. Call for hours. This collection of four 19th century houses, dating from the period immediately before and after the Civil War, are perfectly restored examples of early African-American life in Weeksville. The houses were discovered by historian James Hurley in 1968 when he flew over the area in a small plane and noticed an oddly situated cobblestone street called Hunterfly Road that didn't coincide with the neighborhood's modern street plan.

The four frame houses are the only remnants of the historic Weeksville community and represent a mix of West African hutframing with elements of colonial post-and-beam construction. Owned and operated by the Society for the Preservation of Weeksville and Bedford-Stuyvesant, the homes have been declared historic landmarks and include a small museum on Weeksville history with antique furnishings, period costumes, artifacts and photographs.

Zion Home for Colored Aged Historic Site—Dean Street between Albany and Troy Avenues, Weeksville, Brooklyn. During the late 1800s, this three-story building provided housing for poor elderly African-Americans.

SHOPPING, DINING AND ENTERTAINMENT

African International Market—96 DeKalb Ave., Brooklyn. (718) 260-9078. Hours: Mon.-Sat. 10a.m.-9p.m., Sun. noon-6p.m. An array of Nigerian artifacts and staples including drums, masks, clothing, crafts, jewelry, spices and medicinal powders.

Alemmasha Desta—611 Vanderbilt Ave., Brooklyn. (718) 622-7989. Hours: Mon.-Sat. 10:30a.m.-7p.m. A gift boutique featuring African masks, clothing, hats, walking canes, jewelry and Kente cloth.

Auggie's Brownstone Inn—1550 Fulton St., Bedford-Stuyvesant, Brooklyn. (718) 773-8940. Dinner. One of the oldest African-American owned eateries in Bedford-Stuyvesant, Auggie's is a hole-in-the-wall locals' favorite that features fried chicken, fish and crab dinners.

Bed-Stuy Baker—1407 Fulton St., Brooklyn. (718) 857-7996. Hours: daily 8a.m.-9p.m. A sweet-smelling bakery with fresh baked goods daily and an assortment of piping hot take-out favorites such as barbecue short-ribs, roast turkey and dressing, curried goat, oxtails and cornbread.

Billie Holiday Theater—1368 Fulton Ave., Bedford-Stuyvesant, Brooklyn. (718) 636-0918. Named after the soulful blues singer, this theater stages three major productions a year with a total of about 200 performances. Often called the "theater with a soul and a mission," it is home to one of New York's professional resident black theater groups. The plays, written by African-American playwrights, range from dramas to comedies and musicals, and often get good reviews.

Birdel's Radio & Records—540 Nostrand Ave., Brooklyn. (718) 638-4504. Hours: Mon.-Sat. 10a.m.-7p.m. One of Brooklyn's best record shops when it comes to soul, gospel and oldies records.

Flamingo Lounge—259A Kingston Ave., Bedford-Stuyvesant, Brooklyn. (718) 493-7200. Although it's located in a less than desirable spot, Flamingo is one of Brooklyn's best and least-known jazz clubs. Many of its performers also play at some of Manhattan's finest jazz clubs, and the music is a combination classic cool and modern jazz.

Fountain of Life Restaurant—493 Tompkins Ave., Brooklyn. (718) 783-8547. Lunch and dinner. A casual and friendly eatery specializing in Southern-style home-cooking. Dishes include: smothered steak, oxtails, smothered turkey wings, collard greens, candied yams, squash pie, banana pudding, and fresh fruit punch.

Gage & Tollner—374 Fulton St., Brooklyn. (718) 875-5181. Dinner. Sophisticated and elegant with a mahogany bar, antiques and brass accents. Primarily a steak and seafood eatery, but with a very Southern accent. Established in 1879, Gage & Tollner has become very popular in recent years, mostly because of chef Edna Lewis. A native of Freetown, Virginia, and well past 70-years-old, Lewis has spent a lifetime perfecting Southern specialties using only the freshest ingredients and her meals are a work of art. Lewis has become a bit of celebrity in New York and even has her own cookbook to prove it. Some of her best dishes include: Crabcakes Freetown, shrimp and crab gumbo, grilled pork chops, peach cobbler, and bourbon pecan pie.

Green Avenue Grill—13 Green Ave., Brooklyn. (718) 797-2099. Lunch and dinner. A sleek, family-operated Art Deco cafe with a Kentucky flair and live jazz. Specialties include: smoked ribs, smothered chicken livers, grits and eggs, strawberry pancakes, and pumpkin cheesecake.

Harper Valley Restaurant—745 Fulton Ave., Brooklyn. (718) 596-2367. Lunch and dinner. In the heart of the Fort Green neighborhood, Harper Valley is a simple, seven-table Southern-style restaurant that takes a healthy approach to cooking using more herbs and spices than grease and salt. Dishes include: barbecue chicken, cornmeal coated fried fish, candied yams, okra, and peach cobbler.

Harvest Manor Restaurant—1040 St. Johns Pl., Bedford-Stuyvesant, Brooklyn. (718) 756-0200. Lunch and dinner. This enormous, Southern-style eatery features fried chicken, fish cakes, grits, collard greens, and peach cobbler.

Headstart Books & Crafts—604 Flatbush Ave., Brooklyn. (718) 469-4500. Hours: daily 10a.m.-8p.m. A vast collection of books focusing on the African-American and Caribbean-American experience, a special section for children's and educational books, and a good assortment of African-American posters, cards and gifts.

Keur N Deye Restaurant—737 Fulton St., Brooklyn. (718) 875-4937. Lunch and dinner. Closed Monday. A popular African restaurant specializing in Sengalese cuisine. Dishes include: creamy soups, chicken peanut stew, fish and vegetable stew, sauteed pumpkin and greens.

McDonald's Dining Room—327 Stuyvesant Ave., Brooklyn. (212) 574-3728. Breakfast, lunch and dinner. Established in 1948, this large and comfortable eatery is a neighborhood institution with a Deep South flair. Special dishes include: fried chicken, salmon cakes, short ribs, breaded pork chops, corn bread, and pecan pie.

New Dimension Gallery—767 Fulton St., Brooklyn. (718) 522-7355. Hours: Mon.-Sat 11a.m.-8p.m., Sun. 11a.m.-6p.m. Handcrafted West African creations such as iron-framed chairs covered with mudcloth and Ethiopian fabrics, Nigerian batiks, bronze statues from Benin, and leather hassocks.

New Orleans Cafe—689 Washington Ave., Brooklyn. (718) 398-9800. Lunch and dinner. A friendly neighborhood place featuring authentic Southern and creole cuisine: red beans and rice with sausage, shrimp creole, fried fish, chicken sausage gumbo, and jambalaya.

Nkiru Books—68 St. Marks Pl., near 6th Avenue, Brooklyn. (718)

783-6306. Hours: Sat.-Wed. 11a.m.-7p.m., Thur.-Fri. 11a.m.-9p.m. A jam-packed bookstore full of both rare and best-selling books relating to African-Americans as well as unique greeting cards and children's games.

North Carolina Country Kitchen Restaurant—1993 Atlantic Ave., Brooklyn. (718) 498-8033. Breakfast, lunch and dinner. This handsome, country-style eatery offers classic Southern cooking: slab bacon, grits, honey-baked ham, country pudding, pork barbecue, chitlins, blackeyed peas, pickled okra, hominy grits, cornbread, and sweet potato pie. Across the street is the North Carolina Country Store where you can buy Southern ingredients and spices used in the restaurant.

Paul Robeson Theater—40 Green Ave., Queens. (718) 783-9794. Named in honor of the actor and social activist, the Paul Robeson theater is a cultural center that serves the African-American community. Formerly a Polish Catholic Church, the theater offers a wide range of entertainment including drama, dance and musical productions throughout the year.

Sheila's Place Restaurant—271 Adelphi St., Brooklyn. (718) 935-0292. Dinners nightly and brunch on Sunday. A cozy and sophisticated brownstone setting with an antique mahogany bar, romantic lighting and live jazz. Soul food and Cajun specialties: barbecued pork ribs, smothered chicken, Cajun snapper. Reservations suggested.

Spike's Joint—1 S. Elliot Pl., Fort Green, Brooklyn. (718) 802-1000. Hours: Mon.-Sat. 10a.m.-7p.m., Sun. noon-6p.m. Movie director and marketing genius Spike Lee's boutique is the place to find movie memorabilia, Malcolm X hats, post cards, Kente cloth vests, leather bomber jackets, and trendy, African-American treasures. Since its opening in 1990, Spike's Joint has become a popular tourist attraction drawing young black tourists from as far away as London.

Thelma Hill Performing Arts Center—30 3rd Ave., room 602,

Brooklyn

Brooklyn. (718) 875-9710. A performing arts center that hosts various contemporary and traditional African dance performances.

Chapter 5

Queens

The largest in size of all of the boroughs, Queens makes up over one-third of New York City's total area. As a bedroom community of Manhattan, it is a haven for the middle-class with the highest median income of any borough, and over 300,000 one- and two-family houses. Queens is also the home of Shea Stadium, 6,000 acres of parks, two racetracks, Rockaway Playland, LaGuardia and Kennedy Airports, a booming film industry, and one of America's most well-known bigots—Archie Bunker.

In 1639, the area that today is Queens was purchased by the Dutch from the Rockaway Indians who originally inhabited the land. About 50 years later, when the British took title to the former Dutch colony, it was named Queens in honor of Queen Catherine of Braganza. A pastoral region of rolling meadows, rocky beaches, and broad marshes, Queens remained a sparsely populated agricultural settlement until the early 1900s. During the 1920s and '30s, the population blossomed due to the building of bridges, tunnels and the expansion of the rapid transit system.

Following World War II, Queens experienced a great burst of growth. Compared to the other boroughs it was relatively young and was spared from many of the urban problems that had already taken hold in other parts of New York. It represented great opportunities for residential planners and soon rows and rows of monotonous housing developments monopolized the landscape. Because of its size—118 square miles—and an 1851 law that prohibited further burials in Manhattan, Queens also became the final resting place for many New Yorkers; over a dozen cemeteries are now scattered throughout the borough.

Although the African-American community of Queens can't compare in size to that of Brooklyn's, the neighborhoods of St. Alban's and Corona have substantial middle-class black populations, and many prominent African-Americans at one time or another have lived in the borough, among them: Count Bassie, Billie Holiday, Ella Fitzgerald, Louis Armstrong, Ralph J. Bunche, Jackie Robinson, Malcolm X, and James Brown. And it was in Queens that the late tennis champion Arthur Ashe made sports history by becoming the first black to win the U.S. Open.

Today, visitors in search of African-American history can find in Queens such points of interest as the gravesites of composer Scott Joplin and inventor Granville T. Woods, an obscure black burial ground that dates back to the 1800s, Louis Armstrong's home and museum, and the television studio where the filming of the "Cosby Show" took place.

HISTORIC SITES AND CULTURAL CENTERS

African American Museum of Nassau County—110 N. Franklin St., Hempstead, Long Island (About 15 minutes from Queens). (718) 572-0730. Hours: Tues.-Sat 9a.m.-5p.m., Sun. 1-5p.m. Permanent and rotating exhibits tracing the culture, history and contributions of Long Island's African-Americans. Exhibits include art, books, manuscripts, and occasional exhibits on loan from the Smithsonian Institute.

Aims of Modzawe—115-62 Sutphin Blvd., Queens. (718) 528-

6279. A cultural center offering lectures and workshops on African dance, music, history, language and the visual arts.

Allen AME Church—111-54 Merrick Blvd., Queens. (718) 526-3510. One of the oldest black churches in Queens, Allen AME dates back to the 1830s. The congregation of over 6,000 is actively involved in social service programs in the community.

American Museum of the Moving Image—36-01 35th Ave., Queens. (718) 784-0077. Hours: Tues.-Fri. noon-4p.m., Sat. noon-6p.m. Located across the street from Kaufman Astoria Studios, home-base for much of New York City's film industry, the American Museum of the Moving Image is devoted to the history and art of motion pictures, television and video. A combination working studio and museum, it includes movie sets, sound effects machinery, film memorabilia, and costumes. It once served as the setting for the filming of the "Cosby Show."

Black Arts National Diaspora—143-14 Lakewood Ave., Queens. (718) 657-1168. The Black Arts National Diaspora is a multi-service organization created primarily to assist black artists and Africans. It sponsors art exhibitions, performing arts presentations, art internships, and referral services.

Black Spectrum Theater—Roy Wilkins Park, 119th Avenue and Merrick Boulevard, Queens. (718) 723-1800. A performing arts center specializing in African-American theatrical productions and jazz concerts. Performances at various locations throughout Queens.

Granville T. Woods Gravesite—St. Michael's Cemetery, 72-02 Astoria Blvd., Queens. (718) 278-3240. An African-American inventor who dropped out of school when he was 10-years-old, Granville T. Woods was described during his lifetime by an Ohio newspaper as "the equal, if not the superior, of any living inventor." In direct competition with the famed inventor Thomas A. Edison, Woods was sued several times by Edison. Each time Woods established his right in the U.S. Patent Court to patents or inventions that Edison claimed as his own. In an effort to stifle Woods' rise to fame,

Edison offered him a well-paying job in his laboratory, but Woods turned down the offer and continued to successfully market his own inventions.

Among Woods' many inventions were the train system's "third rail," the electric distributor, the electric safety cutout—a method for sending telegraph messages between moving trains—and a system for sending as many as 200 telegraph messages over a single wire in opposite directions. Woods also invented devices that made railroad travel safer, and by the beginning of the 1900s, every Bell telephone in the United States used his transmitter. Woods died in 1910.

Historic African-American Burial Ground—Everett P. Martins Field, 46th Avenue at 164th Street, Flushing, Queens. This tiny public park served as the Colored Cemetery of Flushing for much of the 1800s. In 1992, following the unearthing of the black burial ground in Manhattan, a retired Broadway singer named Mandingo Osceola Tshaka came to the rescue of this Queens site.

As the Department of Parks was about to begin a $1.2 million dollar renovation of the park, Tshaka came forward with evidence suggesting that hundreds of people may have been buried on the site until a period following the Civil War. Following the war the Colored Cemetery deteriorated into a weed-covered abandoned lot until the city acquired it in 1913, and later turned it into the Everett P. Martins Field park. After Tshaka rallied city officials into stopping the renovation and preserving the burial ground, the Department of Parks agreed to halt the renovation.

Jamaica Arts Center—161-04 Jamaica Ave., Queens. (718) 658-7400. A multi-disciplinary and multi-cultural visual and performing arts center, that is the pride and joy of Queens. A year-round series of performances includes jazz, reggae, and Afro-Asian ensembles.

Kaufman Astoria Studios—34-12 36th St., Astoria, Queens. (718) 392-5600. Established in 1919, Kaufman Astoria Studios is one of the most successful film-making studios outside of Los Angeles. In its early years it employed many great stars including Rudolf Valentino, the Marx Brothers, and African-American actor Paul Robeson.

Langston Hughes Library and Cultural Center—102-09 Northern Blvd., Queens. (718) 651-1100. Hours: Mon., Fri. and Sat. 10a.m.-6p.m., Tues.-Thur. 1-6p.m. A multi-purpose library that also features a Black Heritage Reference Center, art programs, classes and Kwanzaa celebrations.

Louis Armstrong's Residence and Archives—34-56 107th St., Corona, Queens. (718) 478-8274. Tours of the house by appointment only. The famed New Orleans-born jazz artist "Satchmo" resided here in this red-brick building from 1943 until his death in 1971, the longest time he spent in one place. The house was bought by his wife, Lucille, who decided that Armstrong needed a comfortable place to come home to after touring and staying at hotels. Armstrong often sat on the front steps with his trumpet and entertained the neighborhood children. And on every Fourth of July, Armstrong's birthday, he and his wife hosted a huge picnic in the backyard, and invited the neighbors and fellow musicians to join the party.

Following Lucille's death in 1983, the house was turned into a museum of Armstrong's career. Furnished with antiques, it remains exactly the way it was when he and his wife lived there, and includes dozens of instruments, tapes of television shows and radio programs, photographs, music memorabilia, and a small collection of Armstrong's personal letters and original sheet music. It is now owned by Queens College and is listed on the National Register of Historic Places. Each year the college sponsors a jazz festival in Armstrong's honor.

Ralph J. Bunche Residence—115-125 Grosvenor Rd., Queens. This was the Kew Gardens home of noted African-American scholar and diplomat Ralph J. Bunche. In addition to serving as the U.N. Secretary General's representative, Bunche conducted research with

Swedish sociologist Gunnar Myrdal on race relations in America, and in 1950 was the first black awarded the Nobel Prize for Peace.

Roy Wilkins Park—Merrick Boulevard and 119th Avenue, Queens. This small city park was named in honor of the late civil rights leader Roy Wilkins. Community leaders and the Southern Queens Park Association are currently considering turning the area into the Queens African-American Hall of Fame, which if completed, will be a shrine and cultural center in honor of high-achieving blacks with ties to Queens.

Scott Joplin's Gravesite—St. Michael's Cemetery, 72-02 Astoria Blvd., Queens. (718) 278-3240. In 1917 the great ragtime composer Scott Joplin checked into Wards Island hospital because of mental problems. A few days later he died and was buried in this cemetery. In 1974 his grave was marked with a bronze plaque in honor of the revival of his music.

SHOPPING, DINING AND ENTERTAINMENT

Afrikan Poetry Theater—176-03 Jamaica Avenue, Queens. (718) 523-3312. Hours: daily 10a.m.-10p.m. A non-profit community organization that offers an ever-changing array of multi-cultural programs including jazz ensembles, art shows, dance classes, poetry readings, lectures, films, and traditional African story-telling performances. Established in 1976, the ensemble performs throughout New York City.

American Roots Art Gallery—193-17 Linden Blvd., Queens. (718) 712-4141. Hours: Mon.-Fri. 10a.m.-6p.m., Sat. 10a.m.-1p.m. Owned and operated by craftsman David Hodge, this gallery holds an ecclectic collection of first-edition prints, paintings, nostalgic photographs, sculptures and crafts. Also for sale are rare collector pieces by Romare Bearden, Varnette Honeywood and Ernie Barnes.

In addition, owner Hodge is a trained appraiser with a great deal of experience with African-American art.

House of Million Earrings—169-17 Jamaica Ave., Queens. (718) 297-7950. Hours: Mon.-Sat. 9a.m.-6p.m. African clothing and books, and splendid array of hand-crafted, one-of-a-kind earrings.

LaDente—23-4 94th St., East Elmherst, Queens. (718) 458-2172. Lunch and dinner. A friendly, festive and very popular dining room with background piano music and excellent Creole specialties including: curried shrimp and chicken, conch creole, rice and peas, plantains, dumpling stews, and mango chutneys.

Manhattan Proper—217-01 Linden Blvd., Queens. (718) 341-2233. Dinners till past midnight. A trendy and lively restaurant and bar with live jazz and R&B on weekends. Featuring a Continental menu with some Southern specialties: Cajun shrimp, pork chops and cornbread stuffing, thick barbecue ribs, and calves' liver sauteed with brandy and onions.

Chapter 6

Staten Island

*F*or the three million tourists a year who take the half-hour ferry ride past Ellis Island and the Statue of Liberty, Staten Island is the end of the line that few ever venture beyond. The third largest borough in area, but the smallest in population—less than 400,000—Staten Island is about fourteen miles long by seven miles wide. Once a sleepy fishing village where the streets were paved with oyster shells, Staten Island remains a relatively tranquil community. Primarily suburban in atmosphere, it is dotted with dozens of restored historic mansions, unimpressive track housing developments, and marinas that bustle with activity.

Although the African-American population is small, the African-American history of the island is surprisingly colorful. During the Revolutionary War, while the British were in control of New York, three British soldiers attacked an African-American Staten Islander named Bill Richmond. A strong and brawny man with a nimble boxing talent, Richmond managed to single-handedly fight off the three and escape. The incident brought Richmond to the attention of the Duke of Northumberland who was an ardent boxing fan. When the war ended, the Duke brought Richmond to London where he became a prominent figure in sports. In later years, Richmond coached and trained Tom Molineaux, an African-American who became the first unofficial heavyweight boxing champion of the U.S.

During the Civil War, Staten Island served as a military training ground and many of the island's residents were Confederate supporters. When the draft riots of 1863 erupted, abolitionist Horace Greeley sought refuge in Staten Island. Although angry mobs of Confederate supporters tried desperately to kill him, he survived by hiding out in the homes of his Staten Island friends. The mobs also pillaged and burned many buildings, and launched a series of violent attacks against blacks whom they considered to be the cause of the war.

Throughout the Civil War, many Southerners, both black and white, fled the raging South for the safety of Staten Island. The whites settled into boarding houses and small hotels, and the blacks established the Staten Island community of Sandy Ground, known then as the "Gateway to Freedom." Originally established in the Prince's Bay area, the community moved to the area called Sandy Ground when the bay's oysterbeds began to fail and a better location was necessary to earn a living. For a while, the area was called "Little Africa." Sandy Ground today still has a substantial African-American community. Several historic African-American sites in the area have been preserved by the Sandy Ground Historical Society, and many of the people who live in Sandy Ground are descendants of the original black settlers.

HISTORIC SITES AND CULTURAL CENTERS

Baymen's Houses—559, 565, 569 Bloomingdale Rd., Sandy Ground, Staten Island. During the late 1800s, these small, clapboard homes were owned by the more prosperous African-American baymen and oystermen of Sandy Ground. According to historians, the baymen who lived here gathered outside when ever the tide was right for harvesting and sang songs on their way to work. The Sandy Ground Historical Society has plans to restore the houses which are currently owned by the island's AME Zion Church.

Bishop Forge Historic Site—1448 Woodrow Rd., Sandy Ground, Staten Island. Although destroyed by a fire in 1982, the remains of Bishop Forge hold historical significance for Sandy Ground. Founded in 1886, the forge was an important iron works for all of Staten Island. It produced materials for many public buildings throughout New York City, and was the only privately owned blacksmith shop in the city when it was destroyed. Owned and operated by the African-American Bishop family for almost 100 years, the forge also supplied tools for the oystermen of Sandy Ground. The Sandy Ground Historical Society currently owns the forge property and is planning to establish their headquarters and a museum on the site.

Esther V.J. Purnell's Residence—589 Bloomingdale Rd., Sandy Ground, Staten Island. During the oystering days of years ago, this little red and white house was the home of Esther V.J. Purnell. An African-American teacher, Purnell founded a school in this house and took on the responsibility of teaching both the adults and children of Sandy Ground how to read and write.

George Hunter's Residence—575 Bloomingdale Rd., Sandy Ground, Staten Island. George Hunter was one of the more interesting African-Americans in the neighborhood in the early 1900s. His house was always full of neighbors who came by for the home-made cakes, cookies and pies he served to guests. In 1956 *New Yorker* magazine ran a story about Hunter called "Mr. Hunter's Grave." While touring the Sandy Ground cemetery with the reporter, Hunter pointed out the site where he wanted to be buried with his first wife. His second wife, Hunter told the reporter, was far too strong-willed for him to spend eternity with. Unfortunately, Hunter's wishes were not realized and he is buried beside his second wife in the Sandy Ground cemetery.

Issac Harris' Residence—444 Bloomingdale Rd., Sandy Ground, Staten Island. Issac Harris was the son of Silas Harris, an African-American who settled in Sandy Ground in the early 1800s. Although he worked as a servant here, Issac Harris was so well regarded by his employer, the architect Stanford White, that White designed this gambrel roofed home in 1906 and dedicated it to Harris.

"Pop" Pedro's Residence—587 Bloomingdale Rd., Sandy Ground, Staten Island. William "Pop" Pedro, born in 1881, was the unofficial historian and honorary mayor of Sandy Ground. Pop lived to be 106 and until two weeks before his death conducted historic walking tours of Sandy Ground while telling stories about life in the late 1800s.

Rossville AME Zion Church—584 Bloomingdale Rd., Sandy Ground, Staten Island. (718) 356-0200. Founded in 1850, this church has been the center of activity for Sandy Ground's African-American community for over 100 years. During the late 1800s, families gathered here for music, dinners, speeches and prayers in celebration of a free life. Services are still held.

Sandy Ground—One of the oldest "free black" communities in the United States, Sandy Ground is an historic African-American neighborhood in the southwestern corner of Staten Island. Originally established in the Prince's Bay area of Staten Island, Sandy Ground in the mid-1800s served as the gateway to freedom for many blacks from the South.

Sandy Ground Cemetery—Crabtree Avenue, Sandy Ground, Staten Island. Hidden among the sassafras are tombstones dating back to the 1880s. Many of Sandy Ground's earliest African-American residents are buried here.

Sandy Ground Historical Society—1538 Woodrow Rd., Staten Island. (718) 317-5796. A non-profit organization dedicated to the preservation of historic Sandy Ground.

Staten Island Historical Society—441 Clarke Ave., Staten Island.

(718) 351-1611. Hours: July and August, Wed.-Fri. 10a.m.-5p.m., Sat.-Sun. 1-5p.m.; Sept.-June, Sat.-Sun. 1-5p.m. Permanent and rotating exhibits on the history of Staten Island.

Staten Island Museum—75 Stuyvesant Place, (Wall Street), Staten Island. (718) 727-1135. Hours: Tues.-Sat. 10a.m.-5p.m., Sun. 1-5p.m. A small museum with a varied permanent collection on Staten Island history, natural landscape, fine and decorative arts. Included in the museum is "The Black Man on Staten Island," a rich archival collection of photos, manuscripts and oral histories on tape of Staten Island's historic African-American community.

Statue of Liberty—Ferry departures from lower Manhattan 24-hours a day. (212) 269-5755. One of the most famous landmarks in the world, the queen of New York Harbor is remotely connected with two significant events in African-American history. In 1859, John Brown, a white man who seized a government arsenal at Harper's Ferry in an effort to free the slaves, was captured, convicted of treason and executed. After the execution, the French author Victor Hugo started a collection to pay for a gold medal which was then presented to John Brown's widow.

A few years later, when Abraham Lincoln was assassinated, the French again raised money for a gold medal that was presented to Mrs. Lincoln. Part of the inscription on this medal read "He saved the Union without veiling the statue of liberty." One of the people who observed the enthusiasm of the French in raising money for gifts was a sculpture named Auguste Bartholdi. The phrase "statue of liberty" inspired Bartholdi and he became a leader in the plan to present the "Liberty Enlightening the World" statue to the United States.

These two events, John Brown's raid and Lincoln's assassination, both crucial in African-American history, paved the way for the collection of money for the creation of the Statue of Liberty.

Chapter 7

Special Information

TOUR OPERATORS

A Rose in Harlem, (212) 988-6957. Customized tours of Harlem and the South Bronx featuring soul food dinners, jazz and gospel music. Groups of at least 10.

Backstage on Broadway, (212) 575-8065. Behind the scenes tours of Broadway shows.

CityWalks: Walking Tours of New York, (212) 989-2456. Historic walking tours of neighborhoods including Harlem, Greenwich Village, and Downtown.

Dillon Enterprises International, (212) 505-5110. Sightseeing tours for large groups including Broadway theater, jazz and dinner, swing and big band.

Gray Line Tours, (212) 397-2600. Narrated bus tours include Upper New York and Harlem, an evening jazz tour, and the Sunday Harlem Gospel Tour featuring stops at the Apollo Theater, the Schomburg Center, Striver's Row, Morris-Jumel Mansion, and a Southern-style soul food brunch. Available in English, French, German, Italian and Spanish; June through October.

Guide Service of New York, (212) 489-7155. Multilingual customized tours and itineraries for groups and individuals.

Harlem Renaissance Tours, (212) 722-9534. Event coordinator for Harlem Week. Offers multilingual personalized tours for groups of

128

Special Information

10 or more: Gospel, Harlem's Best Nightclubs, Taste of Harlem, Apollo Theater.

Harlem Spirituals, Inc., (212) 757-0425. Narrated bus and walking tours include: Harlem—historic sites, Apollo Theater, museums, shopping, soul food; gospel—church service and gospel choir concert; soul food and jazz—evening excursion including a soul food dinner and jazz performance. Available in English, French, German, Italian and Spanish.

Harlem, Your Way! Tours Unlimited, Inc., (212) 690-1687 Customized tours for individuals and groups including Sunday gospel, Harlem cultural events, night clubs and jazz, black art galleries and antiques.

Manhattan Memories, (212) 628-9517. Multi-cultural history tours of Manhattan's artists, writers, intellectuals, and radicals. Groups of seven or more.

Manhattan Passport, (212) 832-9010. Narrated bus tours include Harlem spirituals and gospel—historic sites and gospel music at a Baptist church; The Good, the Bad, and the Ugly—covering all five boroughs including stops in Harlem. Also available are customized tours featuring significant African-American sites throughout the five boroughs.

Municipal Art Society, (212) 935-3960. The society's historic walking tour program includes Harlem Highlights tours.

New York City Cultural Walking Tour, (212) 979-22388. Customized, privately escorted walking tours of Manhattan's landmarks and historic sites.

New York My Way! (212) 222-9075. Specialized tours featuring gospel, jazz, food, theater, and churches.

92nd Street Y, (212) 415-5599. Customized, multilingual tours of any neighborhood emphasizing history, culture, politics, and ethnicity. Groups of at least 30.

Pathway to Freedom, (212) 431-0233. Summer walking tours sponsored by the Lower East Side Tenement Museum focusing on the history of the African-American community of 19th century New York. Including Cooper Union, Greenwich Village, the site of the African Grove Theater, and the Negro Burial Ground.

Reclaim the Memories: Black History Tours of Old New York, (212) 299-7011. Walking tours of neighborhoods where blacks lived from the 17th to the 19th centuries: Greenwich Village, City Hall Area, Children's History, Women's History, and tours on historical relations of blacks and Jews.

Take-A-Walk, (212) 686-0356. Cassette-recorded walking tours of New York's historic neighborhoods. Cassette players available.

Talking Tours, Inc., (212) 737-5137. Audio cassette walking tours of Manhattan's places of interest including Harlem. Visitors can stop and start at any point. Cassette players available.

CALENDAR OF EVENTS

JANUARY

Martin Luther King, Jr. Day Concert, (718) 622-4433. An annual concert hosted by the Brooklyn Botanical Garden.

FEBRUARY

Black History Month, numerous events throughout the city the entire month.

Black History Makers Awards, (212) 777-6060. An achievement awards ceremony sponsored by the Associated Black Charities.

After Dinner Opera Company, (212) 477-6212. In honor of Black History Month, the company hosts a series of free African-American heritage performances.

Special Information

Channel 13, month-long special programming of documentaries and talk shows honoring African-Americans.

Dance Theatre of Harlem, (212) 690-2800. The acclaimed dance company performs at home for Black History Month.

Kimberly Gallery, (212) 274-1741. A children's gallery that offers a month-long series of story-telling, readings, puppet shows and special entertainment for Black History Month.

Langston Hughes Awareness Day, (718) 651-1100. Films, poetry readings and concerts sponsored by the Langston Hughes Library and Cultural Center.

Museum of the City of New York, (212) 534-1672. Month-long series of gospel and jazz concerts, and entertainment for Black History Month.

Studio Museum of Harlem, (212) 864-4500. Black History Month celebrations and workshops all month long on art, music and film.

MARCH

Vital Expressions in American Art, (212) 864-4500. An annual event in honor of African-American performing, visual and literary arts.

APRIL

Black Roots Festival, (212) 874-5210. An annual celebration of poetry, drama, and music sponsored by the Frederick Douglass Creative Arts Center.

MAY

Amsterdam Avenue Festival, (212) 595-3625. An upper west side festival stretching from 77th to 92nd Street with food, crafts, music and dancing.

Black World Championship Rodeo, (212) 675-0085. A Harlem rodeo celebration of cowboys and cowgirls with emphasis on African-American Western history.

Dance Africa, (718) 636-4100. An annual festival in celebration of African dance hosted by the Brooklyn Academy of Music.

Martin Luther King, Jr., Memorial Day Parade, (212) 281-3308. An annual parade down 5th Avenue from 45th to 86th Street.

JUNE

Annual Salute to Summer Block Festival, (212) 368-6007. A one-day festival in Harlem's St. Nicholas Historic District with music, food, fashions, entertainment and dance.

Black Expo, (212) 216-2778. One of the largest African-American trade shows in the U.S. usually held at the Jacob Javitz Center.

Jazzmobile, (212) 866-4900. A rolling band-stand founded by jazz pianist/composer Dr. Billy Taylor, the Jazzmobile brings free evening jazz concerts to various parts of the city throughout summer months starting in June. Many of the 70-some concerts are held at Grant's Tomb, 122nd Street and Riverside Drive.

JVC Jazz Festival, (212) 787-2020. A descendent of the Newport Jazz Festival, the JVC Jazz Festival hosts a series of jazz performances throughout the city.

Mount Morris Park Historic Neighborhood House Tour, (212) 424-6200. Open house tours of private homes and architectural walking tours through one of Harlem's most charming residential neighborhoods.

JULY

African Family Day Picnic, (718) 638-4588. A Brooklyn family celebration of African roots sponsored by the African Islamic Mission.

African Street Festival, (718) 638-6700. An African celebration over the 4th of July weekend with international foods, art, music and crafts at Boys and Girls High School Field in Brooklyn, sponsored by the Uhuru Cultural Center.

AUGUST

Annual Black Film Festival, (212) 873-5040. A showcase for the history of black film with dramas, comedies, musicals, and documentaries.

Greenwich Village Jazz Festival, (212) 397-8222. Contemporary and classic jazz at various locations.

Harlem Week, (212) 427-3315. For over 20 years, this two-week celebration of Harlem has fostered a sense of community and pride. It features jazz, blues and gospel concerts, block parties, the Greater New York Pro-Am All Star Basketball Classic, historic walking tours, fashion shows, theater, and arts and crafts displays at various locations throughout Harlem.

Weeksville Summer Family Festival, (718) 756-5250. An annual Brooklyn celebration of Weeksville and Bedford-Stuyvesant history with music, dance, foods, horses and games.

SEPTEMBER

African-American Day Parade, (212) 348-3080. For over 20 years this Sunday parade has marched down Adam Clayton Powell, Jr., Boulevard from 111th to 142nd Street in Harlem with bands, floats and celebrations of African-American culture.

Do the Right Thing Festival, (718) 788-1283. An annual street festival in Prospect Park including dance, music, story-telling, puppet-making, arts and crafts, and ethnic foods.

West Indian-American Day Carnival, (718) 773-4052. A five-day Brooklyn festival of music, dance, foods, arts and crafts in honor of the city's West Indian culture. Drawing over one million participants, the event's grand finale is a spectacular parade of floats down Eastern Parkway on Labor Day.

BLACK NEW YORK

OCTOBER

Ebony Fashion Fair, (212) 397-4500. An annual fashion show featuring American and European designers, held in Hempstead, Long Island.

Expressions Festival, (212) 307-7420. A month-long festival of music, dance and films of Africa, the Caribbean and the United States hosted by the Caribbean Cultural Center.

NOVEMBER

AUDELCO Awards, (212) 534-8776. An acronym for Audience Development Committee, AUDELCO promotes African-American theater and hosts this annual awards show to honor African-American actors, actresses and theatrical productions.

International Black Story-telling Festival, (718) 270-5048. A week-long Brooklyn festival honoring the African story-telling tradition with performers from across America, sponsored by the Association of Black Story-tellers.

Langston Hughes Festival, (212) 690-8116. An annual literary event featuring lectures and symposiums that draws writers and African-American scholars from across the country.

DECEMBER

Boys Choir of Harlem, (212) 749-1717. Annual program.

Chango Celebration, (212) 307-7420. An annual tribute to the Yoruba god of fire, thunder, and lightning featuring an arts fair, and dance, music and theatrical productions from Nigeria, Cuba, and Brazil.

Harlem Christmas Tree Lighting, (212) 870-4325. The annual lighting ceremony and dedication of the Harlem Christmas Tree at the Plaza of the Harlem State Office Building at West 125th Street.

Kwanzaa Celebrations, various celebration locations including:

African Poetry Theater, (718) 523-3312

American Museum of Natural History, (212) 769-5100.

Jamaica Arts Center, (718) 658-7400.

Medgar Evers College, (718) 270-4900.

AFRICAN-AMERICAN ORGANIZATIONS

African-American Culture and Arts Network, (212) 749-4408.

African-American Institute, (212) 949-5666.

Alpha Phi Alpha Fraternity, (212) 283-8336.

Associated Black Charities, (212) 777-6060.

Association of Black Social Workers, (212) 348-0035.

Black and Puerto Rican Legislative Caucus, (518) 455-5347.

Black Memorabilia Collector's Association, (212) 255-1059.

Black Representative Association of New York, (212) 234-1695.

Black Women in Publishing, (212) 772-5951.

Caribbean-American Chamber of Commerce and Industry, (718) 834-4544.

Congress of Racial Equality, (212) 353-8130.

Interracial Council for Business, (212) 599-0677.

Jackie Robinson Foundation, (212) 675-1511.

Kappa Alpha Psi Fraternity, (212) 283-9975.

NAACP, (212) 666-9740.

NAACP Legal Defense and Educational Fund, (212) 219-1900.

National Coalition of 100 Black Women, (212) 947-2196.

National Urban League, (212) 310-9000.

Omega Psi Phi Fraternity, (212) 283-9866.

One Hundred Black Men, (212) 777-7070.

Phelps Stokes Fund, (212) 427-8100.

United Black Church Appeal, (212) 992-5315.

United Negro College Fund, (212) 644-9600.

Zeta Phi Beta Sorority, (718) 455-7962.

THE MEDIA

Newspapers and Magazines

The Amsterdam News, (212) 932-7400. The oldest African-American owned newspaper in New York City, the *Amsterdam News* is a thick weekly full of local, national, and international news, arts and entertainment.

The Big Black Book, (718) 638-9223. A useful directory listing African-American owned business in New York City.

Big Red News, (718) 852-6001. A Brooklyn-based weekly paper with an African-American perspective.

Black Enterprise, (212) 242-8000. A monthly business magazine with features on finance, business trends, corporate and small business America.

Black Masks, (212) 549-6908. A monthly magazine published September through June specializing in African-American visual and performing arts across America.

Carib News, (212) 944-1991. A weekly paper serving both the West Indian and the African-American community including news, sports, and local events.

Chocolate Singles, (718) 978-4800. A Queens-based magazine featuring articles of interest to African-American singles including travel, entertainment, and personal ads.

The City Sun, (718) 624-5959. A Brooklyn-based weekly paper

often described as philosophically strident and politically irreverent, featuring national as well local news.

Class Magazine, (212) 677-3055. A New York-based magazine featuring lifestyle articles of interest to blacks in the United States, the Caribbean, and Europe.

Daily Challenge, (718) 636-9500. New York City's only daily African-American paper, the Brooklyn-based *Daily Challenge* features news, sports, and local happenings.

Ebony, (212) 397-4500. One of the most-respected, national African-American monthly magazines in the country.

Emerge, (212) 941-8811. A monthly African-American magazine featuring articles of national concern.

Essence, (212) 642-0600. The magazine for "Today's Black Woman."

Jet, (212) 397-4500. bi-weekly, music and entertainment magazine.

Jump, (212) 732-7447. A high quality magazine featuring articles on both national and international cultural scenes.

The New American, (718) 399-2271. Formerly called the *Black American*, this weekly features local news with a helpful movie and entertainment section.

Routes, (212) 627-5241. A weekly guide to African-American culture including art, concerts, theater, restaurants.

Radio

WBLS 107.5 FM, contemporary and classic R&B.

WGBO 88.3 FM, affiliated with National Public Radio, WGBO is one of the largest public jazz stations in the country featuring contemporary jazz and blues 24-hours a day.

WKCR 89.9 FM, affiliated with Columbia University, featuring jazz daily and blues Saturday afternoons and Tuesday nights.

WLIB 1190 AM, an all-talk/news African-American station with live features from the Apollo Theater.

WMCA 570 AM, Saturday morning programs featuring reggae and calypso.

WNYE 91.5 FM, features Monday evening *Hello Africa* program combining traditional and contemporary African music and news.

WQCD 101.9 FM, contemporary jazz favorites.

WWRL 1600 AM, 24-hour gospel station.

Television

America's Black Forum, news oriented talk program hosted by Julian Bond, Sunday at 2p.m. on Channel 7 (ABC).

Ebony/JET Showcase, profiles and interviews of celebrities, Sunday at 5:30a.m. on Channel 7 (ABC).

Like It Is, news-oriented talk show hosted by Gil Noble, Sunday at 1p.m. on Channel 7 (ABC).

McCreary Report, news feature show, Sunday at 11a.m. on Channel 5 (FOX).

Positively Black, news-oriented talk show, Sunday at 8a.m. on Channel 4 (NBC).

Showtime at the Apollo, popular music variety show and amateur talent contest, Saturday at 1a.m. on Channel 4 (NBC).

Tony Brown's Journal, syndicated talk show featuring African-American issues, Saturday at 11a.m. on Channel 13 (PBS).

HELPFUL SOURCES

Bronx Borough President's Office, 851 Grand Concourse, Bronx, NY 10451, (212) 590-3980.

Special Information

Brooklyn Arts Council, 195 Cadman Plaza W., Brooklyn, NY 11201, (718) 625-0080.

Gay and Lesbian Switchboard, Offers information regarding aspects of gay life in New York City, (212) 777-1800.

Harlem Visitors and Convention Association, 1 W. 125th St., Rm. 206, New York, NY 10027, (212) 427-7200.

Mayor's Office for People with Disabilities, 52 Chambers St., Room 206, New York, NY 10007, (212) 566-3913.

New York Visitors and Convention Bureau, 2 Columbus Circle, New York, NY 10019-1823, (212) 397-8222.

Queens Burough President's Office, 120-55 Queens Blvd., Queens, NY 11424, (718) 520-3823.

New York Subway and Bus Travel Routes, (212) 330-1234.

Young Visitors, Offers information on sites of special interest to children, (212) 595-8100.

FURTHER READING LIST

Albion, Robert G., *The Rise of the Port of New York*, New York: Charles Scribner's Sons, 1939.

Anderson, Jervis, *This Was Harlem*, New York: Farrar, Straus & Giroux, 1982.

Bailey, A. Peter, *Harlem Today: A Cultural and Visitors Guide*, New York: Gumbs and Thomas, 1986.

Baldwin, James, *Notes of a Native Son*, Boston: Beacon Press, 1990.

Belden, Ezekiel Porter, *New York—Past, Present and Future*, New York: G.P. Putnam, 1949.

Bird, Christiane, *The Jazz and Blues Lover's Guide to the U.S.*, New York: Addison Wesley Publishing, 1991.

Bontemps, Arna Wendell, *The Harlem Renaissance Remembered*, New York: Dodd Mead, 1972.

Brown, Henry Collins, *The Story of Old New York*, New York: E.P. Dutton and Company, 1934.

Clarke, John Henrik, ed. *Harlem, A Community in Transition*, New York: Citadel Press, 1964.

Clarke, John Henrik, ed. *Harlem, U.S.A.: The Story of a City Within a City*, Berlin: Seven Seas, 1964.

Clarke, John Henrik, ed. *Harlem*, New York: New American Library, 1970.

Fernow, Berthold, ed., *Records of New Amsterdam from 1653 to 1674*, New York: Knickerbocker Press, 1897.

Flick, Alexander C., ed., *The History of the State of New York*, New York: Columbia University Press, 1937.

Goldstone, Harmon H. & Martha Dalrymple, *History Preserved: A Guide to New York City Historic Landmarks and Historic Districts*, New York: Schocken Books, 1976.

Harris, M.A., *A Negro History Tour of Manhattan*, New York: Greenwood Publishing Corporation, 1968.

Haskins, Jim, *The Cotton Club*, New York: New American Library, 1977.

Huggins, Nathan Irvin, *Voices From the Harlem Renaissance*, New York: Oxford University Press, 1976.

Jameson, J. Franklin, ed., *Narratives of New Netherland, 1609-1664*, New York: Charles Scribner and Sons, 1909.

Johnson, James Weldon, *Black Manhattan*, New York: A.A. Knopf, 1930.

Lewis, David L., *When Harlem Was in Vogue*, New York: Oxford University Press, 1983.

Mackay, Ernst A., *The Civil War and New York City*, Syracuse: Syracuse University Press, 1990.

McKay, Claude, *Harlem: Negro Metropolis*, New York: E.P. Dutton & Co., 1940.

Osofsky, Gilbert, *Harlem: The Making of a Ghetto*, New York: Harper, 1971.

Special Information

Plunz, Richard, *A History of Housing in New York City*, New York: Columbia University Press, 1990.

Schoener, Allen, ed. *Harlem On My Mind: 1900-1968*, New York: Random House, 1968.

Ulmann, Albert, *A Landmark History of New York*, New York: D. Appleton-Century Co., 1939.

VanDerZee, James, *The World of James VanDerZee: A Visual Record of Black Americans*, New York: Grove Press, 1969.

Wesley, Charles H., "The Negroes of New York in the Emancipation Movement," *Journal of Negro History* XXIV, Jan., 1939.

Index of Sites